Truth to Triumph

A Spiritual Guide to Finding Your Truth

Lily Sanders

ABL Publishing

New York, New York

ABL Publishing
71 Broadway
New York, N.Y. 10006

Book Cover Design by Trevor Lorkings
Photography by Todd Weisman

Truth to Triumph / Lily Sanders
1st edition.
ISBN 978-0-9993245-0-9 (HC)
ISBN 978-0-9993245-1-6 (SC)

Library of Congress Cataloging in Publication Data
Library of Congress Control Number: 2017911223

Dedication to my son.

Always remember how perfect and significant you are in the canvas of this Universe.

—LILY SANDERS

Table of Contents

Author's Introduction

I've been writing this book for three years….inside my head.
My biggest fear of putting words on paper was exposing
others to my secrets. I stored my secrets in a locked up box
inside my head, in hopes that one day these memories would
somehow dissipate into thin air along with the pain they
carried. That hope was never realized. What did happen was
that I had a life changing awakening. Eventually, I felt a
strong pull, which was much more than a mere tug, to write
about how we can spin thread into gold. How we can take
all of the minutiae in life situations, and use them as positive
transformation in our lives. Most people have mastered the
use of small, trifling matters by creating mountains of
pointless suffering from them. Then there are the seemingly
denser life situations that bring pain. What I found was that
pain was not my individual burden. We all experience pain.
Everyone on this planet at some level or another has
experienced loss, sudden change, and various drastic life
circumstances where the impact of it all have been extreme.
The pain that we encounter from these circumstances and the
challenges that arise from them are necessary for us to

evolve. So it is safe to suggest that pain can be useful, as long as we understand how to transmute it into peace and triumph over adversities in our life situations. The suffering, however, serves no purpose other than to make you unhappy. The one thing I know now is that we create our own suffering. We manifest it by our resistance to what is, and our need to keep the commentary in our minds not only alive, but readily available for protection, and even combat. We store them as unhappy stories that we categorize and pull from when we feel the emotional need to do so. Although you do not talk about your unhappy stories, does not mean you have let them go. In fact, what I found is that many of us have volumes of stories conveniently stacked in the bookshelves of our mental library that we reach for every time we choose to suffer. When we have forgotten our truth, we suffer. As I began to write this book, I felt compelled to explain how pain can be used for growth, and how suffering can end by changing the conditioning of our mind, and improving and raising our level of consciousness. This is not a positive thinking book, rather it is a book that will challenge readers to tune out the thinking mind, and tune into an innate mind, if you will, that has the potential to see and live life at a much deeper level, where their truth guides them into the manifestation of great and mighty things. These pages are filled with a collage of true and raw stories, insightful messages, and spiritual undertones that come together as a symphony of inspiration and triumph. I trust that these chapters will help men, women, and children learn to let go of their own unhappy stories and release their self-identification as a victim. Even the most incomprehensible acts such as deprivation, emotional, mental and physical abuse, and acts of violence cannot take your truth away. The intention of this book is to show readers how we get caught up in unconscious living, the damaging effects it has on us, what can be done about it, and why it is critical for our overall well-being to make a conscious shift into awareness. We have so much potential on this planet as a human race to break the mold for generational blessings, one person at a time, one family at a time, and one life at a time. I dedicate this book to my son who has been such a gift in my path, and my reason for questioning the true meaning of life. It was in that quest that I discovered an opening into my own evolution, where the answer began to beautifully unfold.

The intent of this book is to teach others how to rise above and learn from their personal life experiences. I am not a psychiatrist or psychologist but have journeyed through enough life experiences that have ultimately become a doorway into my new path as a spiritual teacher. That said, read with an open heart and a clear mind. One never knows what one can learn on this earth on any platform. So I invite you to avail yourself to the pages before you and know that I love you.

Truth to Triumph

A Spiritual Guide to Finding Your Truth

Lily Sanders

The Grass Blades in Cement

IN THE SERVICE OF LOVE, it has been said that only the wounded can serve. And since there is not one person on this earth that has not been wounded, we are all capable of bringing healing to one another. First to one's self. It has taken me nearly five decades to personally embrace love for myself, forgiveness for those who've scorned me, and courage to share some of my secrets. These secrets have collected in my mind for the past years and have finally crept forward, pen in hand, to land the surfaces of these pages, in trust that it will help others transcend their own pain, and impact lives in most immeasurable ways.

One gloomy day, a short time after my first love had dropped into and then fallen out from my young life, had reappeared to my surprise, as an unsolicited messenger. He delivered a large bouquet of wilted, dead flowers to an address for a particular gentleman who was at the crossroads of my life at the time. A mysterious hand written note was pinned to the red ribbon that wrapped the box of curiosity with perfection. Days later, the recipient shared that he had received an interesting box from a florist, delivered by a man of few words, and on it, was a tiny note. The note read: 'You can kill a lily, but she will always come back to life.' I imagined that the deliverer took it upon himself to author this message, and place it on the box in which the wilted flowers were packaged. I suppose he might have acted differently if the gentleman had behaved better in the situation he had just learned about. Looking back, I realize how profound that statement was. I found it to be quite figurative language scripted on that tiny note. It's interesting to me how I've carried those words on that note inside my heart for a good part of more than twenty-five years. 'You can kill a lily, but she will always come back to life'. They were a spiritual life saver to me at times when the skies would darken well after the sun had risen. I tell some of my stories within these pages to shed some light on those who are currently in a dark place. We would not be human if we didn't find ourselves in a dark place at one point or another in life, so this book is for everyone who breathes life. Each person's pain and dark place differ from the next, however, be assured that the common denominator is always the darkness.

I have gratitude for the many blessings in life and know my purpose here. I don't judge past experiences as mistakes because I know they have led me to where I am today...to now. It was the path I took that I eventually used as an opening into awareness and self-growth. Some people call this an awakening or enlightenment. If I were to describe my tenacity, and a strong pull to transcend during these weighted experiences metaphorically, it would be as grass blades in cement that sprout out and lean toward the sun. I struggled to get out from beneath the cement and was left flattened and worn down. One day as I reached toward the sun for energy, I knew in that moment that life was at the roots beneath the cement, and at its core was the infinite I am-ness of who I am. That being said, I am living proof that there is light at every crossing, that there is healing ever so possible, and that love is not prejudiced. Love is for everyone. We are love. Experiencing love depends on our ability to see it and feel it, in oneself and in every living thing. Every person, a tree, an animal, and even a rock are all expressions of loving energy. All of it is part of the Universe that serves us in so many ways, should we choose to accept this in love, honor, and respect. In that acceptance, you can truly live a life that you love.

I will be sharing some of my experiences, all be it personal to me that have been hidden in my secret place. I will share these in fragments, within the next few chapters in order to bring insight, so you can intuitively grasp a deeper understanding of how peaceful transformations can be applied in your own life. I acknowledge experiences around the globe and honor the world's pain, which is one of the reasons why this book was written. My passion is for humanity and to become a light that burns up the nonsense in life, which I often refer to as minutiae. My goal is to encourage you to let go of your own unhappy story and live for today, creatively building upon and growing in a present life filled with love, honor, and respect for oneself and toward others. You can manifest a life you love.

I trust that the messages you receive while reading this book are that of inspiration. Without knowing any of your personal experiences, I do know that they can be opportunities for your own personal awakenings. I have learned that the ideal situation in life is one that provides you with challenges. And yes, these challenges may come with a lot of pain. But without that, there would be no awakening. Life is meant to be challenging. It is how the Universe works, in its process of naturally pushing us to evolve. Challenge is what forces evolution to happen, and with these challenges there is change. Change is an inevitable necessity for growth. We need it. Imagine if you were to have a stagnant life? You can compare that to a still reservoir of water, where growing mold and bearing unpleasant smells were its only consequence. Just as a body of stagnant water becomes foul from standing, so would we. We need the constant flow of moving waters. It is within these currents that we learn how to navigate through life.

As overwhelming some waves seem, you can truly learn to use that energy for dynamic outcomes. Nearly twenty years ago, I was literally drowning in the beautiful waters of Bermuda. Strong currents were hauling me back and throwing me sideways away from the shore as I was snorkeling. When I looked up over the waves that were pulling me, I saw that I was no longer snorkeling in the lagoon, but had been dragged outside of the lagoon even further from the shore. It was frightful. The cold salty water swam through my nose and flowed down my throat. Fear set in as the weakness in my muscles were competing with the rapid beat of my heart. I had two decisions to make within seconds. Give up and drown, or stop fighting the waves and start using them to save me. I made a decision and changed my course of action. I replaced my fear with a state of acute attention. I became very present. Having never experienced anything like this, innate kicked in as I observed the motions of the current that was surrounding me. I began to swim into and along the waves, using its enormous force of energy to naturally push me toward the shore at each of its thrusts. I used the force and energy of the waves for my benefit. It was an aha moment of survival. There was a knowing of life in that present moment. Once I let go of the fear, which is always in the thinking mind, I was safe. I wound up back on the sand. As I laid on my back on the sandy shore, the energy of the sun began to warm and dry my skin. It was comforting. What was equally comforting was discovering my swim suit still intact and covering all areas of concern. At that moment I was breathing and still looking decent. What more could I ask for? That subtle internal laughter reminded me how each moment is new in its own experience, each breath was a new awakening, and how each thought carries its own sense of humor. This experience was real and is no different than how we can treat all challenges that are thrown our way.

Having said that, the following stories I will be sharing will deliver self-expression as to how I surrendered to the waves, metaphorically speaking, and how I learned to swim proficiently and experience life below the ocean's surface. When you can let go of the resistance to what is, and surrender to it, you will begin to live life at a much deeper level. Surrender is not weakness. Surrender is coming into presence, which holds power in the only thing that truly matters. This moment. When I speak of surrender, I speak of giving in to your innate ability to not only survive a situation but more importantly to thrive because of it. I will write more about this as you turn the pages, but for now, I invite you to receive my contribution of these secret stories, which I have mindfully written in love and truth, by using it to bridge the gap between where you are today, and where the purpose in your life awaits.

The Added Story

Initially, I imagined this book might be a compilation of some memoirs, and poems that I've written in somewhat chronological order that would give you glimpses into the secrets and wounds I had carried. For a brief moment, I felt it would be paramount for me to uncover these truths, as ugly as they may be judged. Something was still unsettling inside of me, however. I acted on intuition and got still. I wanted to determine why telling these stories would be paramount. Would it be paramount for me, or for my readers? I wanted to be certain that the stories I chose to reveal in this book are written to serve others, and not in the service of my ego, or the collective ego for that matter. I used to believe that truth can encompass the tragic flaws in life...within ourselves, within others, and in different experiences, we've encountered. However, what I discovered in the past few years was that truth is not found in stories. The events and happenings are in the past. Even yesterday's experience is the past. The stories are what we add to our experience. The stories may be relatively true, but they are not your truth. They cannot diminish your truth in any way. The only thing that is absolute is your truth.

What do I mean by this? What is absolute is pure. It is complete in its independence from any experience, happenings or events. It is what arises in its own space after the exhale of an experience. Yes, these stories I will be sharing are true. However, I intend to uncover the absolute secrecy about these stories. We will look at the truths hidden and covered beneath the layers of these stories. I will not just unfold what is relatively true but will explode the underlying nuances that were realized after these different experiences. That realization is consciousness. As most of our stories involve deep hurt from a past event, I wanted to remove that part from the story and look at the reality of what was left. In doing this, what was left was the event without the judgmental commentary that is stored in the mind. Basically, it is the event without the hurt and judgment added to it. What I found was that most hurt stems from our feelings of being diminished, betrayed, or let down by someone or some circumstance that we expected different behavior from or a different outcome with. Then we add our judgment on top of it by thinking what should have been said, or what could have been done, and so on. A sense of love, trust, and loyalty suddenly dissolves and leaves you feeling cut. Wounded. Empty. Almost like someone just dug a hole into your heart. Sound familiar? We tend to feel this on a personal level, and also collectively as a human race when we forget who we really are.

The reality of a story that happened is what occurred at that particular time, during the level of conscious awareness at the time that it happened. That pretty much sums it up. If we could put a full stop at the end of this, we would be a lot better off. This is easier said than done for most of us. How an event emotionally affects us, is what has the potential to bring pain. That pain can either evolve us as human beings or cause suffering. When you add your hurt feelings to what has happened, you continue the commentary in your mind and keep re-living it, even way after it has happened. What I found is that some people sweep their story under the carpet as they buy into the humiliation that their ego is selling them, while others may tend to constantly talk about it. Some people will tell their story out loud, talking to no one really. They speak what is in their mind, out loud, void of any vocal filter. In many cases, this is known as schizophrenia. It is widely known as a mental disorder. At one point or another when we experience feelings of hurt, betrayal, fear and worry, don't we all break down internally to some degree and get caught up between our thinking mind and our emotions? Do you ever catch yourself reacting and behaving according to those internal feelings? Of course, you do. The only difference between that and schizophrenia is that most of us have the ability to suppress or hide those disturbances in the mind and emotions, where it does not affect external life situations, circumstances, or relationships. Or does it? Is it possible to consider that all of the emotional pain you carry is all an illusion of thought? Instead of a noticeable deterioration in the level of functioning in everyday life, as in schizophrenia, the real loss of contact is with the present moment. And so you go on telling your story to yourself inside your head, forming gulfs between relationships, families, and even races. But the great loss is that gulf you form between you and your Self. Your truth. You do this because of things that happened behind this moment, and illusory thoughts of the next moment. I call this acceptable schizophrenia, or acceptable unconscious living, where there is a disconnect between your mind and your natural self, which is considered normal. Or at the very least, you are not considered crazy. Many people, even countries carry their stories and plan their revenge and retribution for years on end. Many times, this turns into the victim role, where we identify ourselves as a victim. We see this manifest on a personal level and in other individuals across the globe. By identifying with a label I will call the victim, you become a sufferer of this or that or a survivor of this or that. Labeling has become very common and very much acceptable behavior. Perhaps you even introduce your child as one who suffers from autism or a friend who is a cancer survivor. Maybe you introduce yourself as a sufferer or survivor of this or that. I see this all the time. We manifest this victim label in organized groups as well, by establishing and naming them after the very thing that started the pain and caused the suffering. This eventually spins into a collective form of victim roles and labeling, where suddenly you begin to fight the wars of the world. You fight for the cause against this or the cause against that and ego tells you that this is your purpose, and yet, in reality, it is keeping the wound very much alive. Life becomes an open sore hidden and wrapped in a bandage called cause. Cause, however, situates itself either dormant or active at its source. Cause hides at the roots, not in the withering flower after spring has gone. This was a major discovery for me in that I was cognizant of where cause emerged. Cause continues to remind you of the hurt, long after the event has occurred. Many people will take a cause to their grave, or fight for a cause driving others to their grave. Either way is madness in the form of acceptable unconscious living. This unconscious mind set is a learned condition and will keep you in the darkness until you are ready to evolve. An unconscious mind will buy into the drama of yesterday's play and see it as reality when it is really just yesterday's play.

What I learned was that whenever there was intense pain in my life, there was also a possibility for a deep and personal awakening within myself. I felt a force of energy in my pain that had power, and felt that if I could somehow draw from that power and use it in a positive way, I could evolve. I began to see a source of strength arising through pain, even in the faint distance. That strength eventually proved itself and manifested as a light that emerged from beneath the rubble. The rubble from all of life's pitfalls. This unveiling was a powerful discovery for me. Truly, what I found was that I've always possessed this light, but have forgotten it until now. Pain is what jarred my soul's memory and forced me to look deeper. So in my experience, it is safe to suggest that pain has the potential to bring you to that place where rocks can be unturned, and the light exposed. The peace that illuminates from that light, is also the piece that has been missing all along. Welcome home. When I speak of home, I speak of completion. Oneness. Love.

It doesn't matter what happened in your personal life situation, or any occurrences around the globe. The only thing that matters is where you are at this moment. This is not to say that we should not care or have compassion. In fact, compassion for humanity can be extremely powerful in the healing process of oneself and even a country. It has proven to be very effective in my personal life experience. What I am saying, however, is that the added story prolongs the healing process and keeps the wound fresh. Instead, peel off the bandage. Don't add the story to it. Don't buy into the drama. When you do not attach a story to what is, the emotional baggage doesn't arise. It can't arise because there is no judgment there. There is only acceptance. What I found is that where there was an attachment to a story, was a judgment of it. In my personal experience, much of the unhappy commentaries I had stored inside of me, paralleled with my judgment of the past occurrence. Not only did this keep past occurrences alive in my thinking mind, but it also kept my emotional wounds alive. For me, non-judgment was letting go. Once I learned to let go of judgment, the story disappeared too. You are aware you have a wound, but you don't harp on how it got there, and you don't judge how it happened. Now it begins to heal from the inside out. Will you still have a scar? Perhaps. But the idea is to let go of the commentary in your mind so that it no longer has an emotional effect on you. For me, this was life changing. It allowed me to get off of the emotional roller coaster and just be. Be who and what? Just be. Be in life, of life, and with life as I am purposed to be. No more baggage, no more labels, no more victim, no more fears. The only thing that remains is love. Because truly, life is not something we own. It is not your life, your divorce, your illness, your child, or your possessions. In truth, you are life. If you can separate the concept of life from life occurrences, what is left? Truth. Oneness. Love.

Now I know that whatever happened, is behind this moment. A past experience is incapable of stopping my joy in the present moment. And so in this moment, I encourage you to see the grander possibilities of it. When I really grasped this concept, a switch went on and lit up my entire body. It was so logical, yet so foreign to me. This concept enlightened me. Much of the world's population exists in a state of non-presence. When you are thinking of the moment behind or waiting for the moment ahead, you are not in the moment at hand. This non-presence is a state of unconsciousness. That state of being unaware that you are here, and not over there is debilitating.

Choose to be present. Choose to be conscious. This is not rocket science, yet the word itself [conscious] is so widely misunderstood and cannot even be explained by science. In my view, we need to put more importance and emphasis on the concept of being conscious. What does it mean then, to be conscious? To be conscious is to be present. It is not a thing. It is formless. It is timeless, and yet eternal. It is the space, or the nothingness between thoughts if you will. There is tremendous power and freedom in letting go of the added story as you experience your truth in each moment it encompasses. So what is paramount, is the truth of this moment.

You cannot be in this moment if you are associating with the past. It is just not possible. You can also distort the truth by constant identification with whatever the thinking mind tells you. You continue to live out the story that your mind has arranged for you. As a result, you may spin into depression, anger, despair, financial havoc, and so on. All of it leads to one thing. Suffering. What is your mind set in this moment? What does the arrangement of your mind look like? The beautiful magnificence that you have the potential to experience in each moment is not created by some unknown phenomenon. It is manifested by your mind's perception of yourself. In my view, what the mind senses or sees is what you will manifest. The following chapters describe some life events that brought me to my truth and taught me how to triumph over it all.

"Love is a state of being."

~Lily Sanders

CHAPTER 2

First Impressions

ONCE UPON A TIME, there was a young girl, not yet in grade school who recently moved into a small, fairly old home that was still foreign to her. What was not foreign to her were the fables that she listened to every day without fail. That little artistic dreamer was me. I remember lying on the hard wood floor of my mom and dad's bedroom in front of the record player that was to the left of their bed. On my back, knees up and feet anchored to the hard wooden floor, I would stare at the album cover of Cinderella. The characters would begin to come alive in my imagination. Rolling over to my tummy, heels to the ceiling, I grabbed the Bic blue ink pen I saw on the floor beside me and doodled on the album jacket, both front and back, emphasizing all that was in my imagination's eye. The sides of my young hands were covered in blue smudged ink as they swept across the newly inked drawings. I remember being engrossed in this as I engaged with the story, and to that little girl inside, it was all part of the journey of listening, feeling, imagining, and creating. I sang along with Paul Tripp's song. It was an album that told the story of Cinderella by narration, voice over, and music. I knew my way around and through the entire story and lyrics, forward and backward. I could recite every word and sing every song on that album. The album jacket was so worn in with doodled blue ink all over it, and I loved it. It had character. On the cover, Cinderella was so pretty despite her sad, pathetic eyes. As she ran down the staircase from the palace ball in her beautiful gown, the worrisome in her creamy white face befell her. I saw the opposites of fear and courage in her eyes. I heard the love in her outer dialogue and felt love inhabit the wish list in her heart. The illustrations, along with the story and lyrics spoke volumes to me in simultaneous rhythm. Those of you that were raised in the mid to late 60's, or were raising children then, would remember this form of entertainment quite well. To me, this was a form of learning life morals and was to become an opening into manifesting high principals and expressing and conveying truth, only I didn't know it at the time.

I listened to three albums that were all told by Paul Tripp, all different, all fairy tales. But Cinderella was the one that resonated with me after all of these years. The memory of listening to it, again and again, would come and go in my adult life. At fifty-two years of age, in January 2015 that memory wakes me before dawn with the song. The very song I would sing along with when I was such a little girl. I was so impressionable then, so sad, and yet so hopeful. As I lay there awake with my eyes still closed, I begin to sing the tune in my head. The phrases were all there, but not in its proper place. It bothered me that I couldn't remember exactly what they were, so I began to sing it aloud. And there it was!

"The story of Cinderella can come true
For me...and you
Look to the new day
And the happiness that's in it
Even if it's raining
Don't let your dreams fade...not even for a minute..."

This was the theme song. It was played at the beginning of the fairytale, and then under scored at the end of the fairytale. This recollect was a profound moment for me. Seems so silly and juvenile but a deeply seated state of emotion had overpowered me. How enchanting it was to remember the lyrics from forty-eight years ago and feel compelled to sing it aloud before the crack of dawn. Physically shifting from sleeping mode I leaped out from under the pile of blankets and pillows on my sofa and toward my desk to write it down. It struck me in that these lyrics were inspiring, and apparently had been etched in my heart after all of these years. Who knew? On this night I identified with it. At that very moment, I recognized the impact it had on me and felt that it was somehow built into my character. I understood the birth of my tenacity and hope. The very lyrics stamped a distinctive impression on me. Even as a little girl, I was already experiencing the need for hope. I often wondered why. At that time I couldn't place a finger on that answer. Many years later, before I gave birth to my son, I knew the answer to that question and completely understood it. I was aware that young children, babies, and even while in the womb always sense conflict. When they are toddlers they already understand love, lack of love, unity, and division of family. No matter how much you try and hide it, they sense it. They see what they see, and they see what they do not see. They feel what they feel and they feel what they do not feel. They are naturals at it.

The Closet

The frightful thickness of silence in the air became an everyday occurrence after 4:30 pm weekdays, and throughout weekends in our house growing up. That was when my father was home. I loved my father and am grateful for both him and my mother, whom if it weren't for them, I would not be here writing this book. At the time of this event, however, I did feel that if the walls could speak they would cry out for help, for hope, and for peace. On this particular day, the walls did exactly that. My father was in a terrible mood, and all was silent in the house. Four children, a mother, and father and all were silent. The only thing that I remember hearing was the sniffling of my mother from downstairs, and the gate of the stockade wooden fence outside slamming open and shut in the wind. I remember I was about nine or ten. My bed was on the near south wall of the bedroom, and my sister's bed was on the far north wall. Being that she was about four years older than me, we did not do everything together. I don't recall where she was on this day, I only remember that I was in our bedroom alone. My heart was pounding, and I could hear it. The quiet in the walls were frightening. To me, it always represented the silence before the storm. I opened up the closet door to hide in it. I remember the door knob was on the left and I opened it out toward me and went inside. Before I closed the closet door, which was on the east wall, I remember the sun beamed from the west window and lit up the side of the closet. As I looked to my right, that is when the walls cried out. There on the inside of the closet wall, I saw what looked like my sister's handwriting. Each word was desperately penned. It read: *dear God, please help this family.* I read it and tears began to trickle from my eyes. And then they began to stream silently down my face. I closed the door quietly as I tried to turn the knob left and then right, so as not to make a clicking sound at the end of its closing. Until this day, I never spoke of what I saw written in the closet. All I knew was that we possibly shared the same hope for peace and rescue. It was a shame how we endured pain and suffering and didn't even feel comfortable communicating it and supporting each other. After all, we were just kids that didn't understand it, and couldn't even begin to fix it. Are children supposed to grow up with the responsibility or burden of fixing an adult who is their parent and is expected to be of sound mind? Probably not. But the reality is that as long as adults live life at a level of unconsciousness, it does bleed burden and intense pain which can inflict suffering on their children. Many years later, as a young adult, the old house was sold with the little-inscribed prayer along with it, as it remained in the closet for all of those years that I remember growing up.

The Legacy

It was said and judged that my Italian grandfather, who was deceased, was a violent and controlling person. I was told stories of my father's father enjoying urban Sunday summer afternoons with the neighborhood priests, where sipping Italian red wine from stemless glasses and casual conversion was a common event on the stoop of their Bronx apartment. Another event shared was my grandfather throwing the Christmas tree out the window of their building of that same apartment one year, while spectators could still smell my grandmother's sauce across the ally way that had been cooking since morning. I never knew him. What I did know was that there was a pattern that apparently had developed through the generations. It showed environmental similarities that had been passed down. So this was our family legacy. A legacy of undeniable domestic violence. What a rip off I thought. Most children grow up and get the family business or the good china. We got the beatings. That pretty much summed it up for me.

One day one my sister and I went to my Aunt for what we had hoped would be our first courageous time to tell someone outside our immediate family what we were experiencing behind closed doors. We bravely told my Aunt that our father was beating us. We didn't color or add to the story. We just came out with the facts. It was difficult enough to even discuss and expose, and so we didn't give any ugly details. She proceeded to respond in an odd 'matter of fact' way. In my view, I remember the response as unemotional and pragmatic. I don't recall exactly what she said but her reply was something like this: "Our father hit us too. That's what they do. It doesn't mean your father doesn't love you." Astounding remark, I remember thinking. I imagine she may have responded differently if she had a different experience in her own upbringing as a child. Only a few stories were shared and their life as children was seldom spoken of. My hopeful face dropped and my sister was angry. We went to her for help and realized she was not the right candidate for the job. It seemed at the time that no one was. Those days, early 70's, schools and teachers did not discuss, recognize or understand domestic violence. In fact, they turned the other way. Our terror continued.

My father would often line us up as if we were in the army. He would interrogate us on whatever the flavor of the day or week was. Usually, it was when one of us did something that angered him, we all were in jeopardy of a beating or at the very least, the dreadful interrogations that toiled with our minds. My personal memory of it was nothing less than awful.

One day he was interrogating my oldest brother. He asked my brother a question. He was to remain there until he gave an answer. The right answer got you off of the interrogation line up. The reverse usually got you either a beating, or you had to stay standing there until you came up with the answer he wanted to hear. I remember my brother standing there for what seemed to be at least an hour. I imagine that my brother was either afraid of what his first answer might be or if it were the right one, or was contemplating sharing the voice inside of his head to disagree. It was probably the latter. It seemed that he also would day dream off into a mental space of safety, which was actually fear in safety's clothing, while my father awaited an answer, which challenged my father even more. This always led him to an insane result of even worse mental abuse. It was an environment I do not wish on anyone.

Typically in our house growing up, when one sibling was in trouble, we all were in trouble. It's been said that I received the least amount of physical beatings. To my recollection, my oldest brother may have received the most amounts of physical beatings, although memory cannot be certain. However, we were all interrogated on a regular basis for hours at a time, which was emotionally traumatizing. The point is, each of us owned our own personal pain. Collectively, we shared it. I grew to understand this as shared compassion.

The beatings can only be described one way. Our father would take both his hands, the inside palms of them, and pound them on the sides of our head, one firm hand into the right side of our head, and the other firm hand into the opposite side of our head. He did this hard. The ringing in the ears and throbbing head pains were an experience we all shared. My brothers received this form of treatment more so than me and my sister. Often my brothers were taken by their ear, and my sister and I by our hair, and were pulled around the room in that manner as we were reprimanded. By the grace of God, we were spared death. What we were not spared, however, was our dignity. Esteem and worth were not given to us as children. In my view, we were robbed of this natural feeling growing up. It had to be sought after. I later learned as an adult, to stop searching outwardly for it because I already had it inwardly. I just needed to look deep. It was always there, and yet, it took me decades to find it. My mind was programmed by my father, his dictatorship, and the environment I lived in so much so, that I never learned to navigate my own heart until recent years which I discuss later in chapters.

School Days

My father forbade us to be in any sports or after school activities. We were required to come straight home, do our designated chores, and be at the kitchen table washed up, respectfully and conservatively clothed for dinner by the time he came home from work. Everyday. We rarely disobeyed this rule. We skirted around that from time to time to have somewhat of a normal kid life growing up by participating now and again in something after school like a sport, or a school play. There was always a price we had to pay for it though. Aside from a possible punishment or beating, the bigger loss was not having parental support and encouragement to participate and engage in socially accepted activities.

I was in Junior High School, and many of my friends were trying out for cheerleading. I was excited to try out with my friends, and for the moment took no mind to the consequences. I figured I still might be able to get home in time to brush and hang my father's suit when he got home. As it turned out, I made the cheer leading squad and was appointed captain or co-captain. I don't recall, as nothing really was given praise or recognition to growing up. I only know that I was appointed this title because I seemed to have the talent they were looking for. We were given the schedule for rehearsals and told how long the season ran, which was from basketball into football season. This meant late home weekdays, and early out on Saturday mornings. Now what, I thought? My stomach was sick and I remember my body trembling, while the others that made it feeling thrilled, as any Junior High School student might be. When I came home, I went upstairs and signaled my mother into the bathroom for privacy. I told her that I had made the cheerleading squad and was appointed a title that involved choreography. She did not appear to be happy about it. My mother was not capable at the time, to stand up to my father and tell him the truth. I imagine it terrified her just to think about the conflict this might create. None the less, she covered for me as she did with all of us. When I had away games, I would return home when it was dark. That was forbidden in our household. I remember changing behind the girls in the back of the bus, out of my short cheer leading skirt, into pants, because that for sure was a beating guaranteed. Eventually, it wasn't worth the absurd pretense. It brought me nothing more than a sick stomach, anxiety on the bus ride home, and terror as I approached the block my house was on. Having fun and socializing, on the bus ride home with each other and with the guys on the team, was all part of the experience that I could not enjoy. My mind was fixated on the worries of walking in the front door, so I was not able to feel at ease with any of it. It was a charade that kept me from enjoying the moment and it just didn't seem worth it. I couldn't relax and connect with most girls and guys on the bus because the fear outweighed my ability to be happy. To be happy would have required my presence. To be happy would have required my letting go of the thoughts in my mind. I was only a teenager with no real answers. But even at that age, however, I knew that I needed to take some kind of action that would remove fear from the experience. So I eventually decided to quit the squad sometime during football season. I remember telling some of the girls that it was way too cold for me on Saturday mornings on the football field. Although that may have been relatively true, it was not the absolute reason I left the squad. I don't even recall the reason that I gave to the teacher who led the team. All I remember thinking inside my head as I told her, was that my life really sucked. I really liked that teacher, too. All five feet of her. She always smelled like delicious perfume, and I judged her as such a classy woman. She dressed like a lady, and her hair and makeup was always so perfect. She wore large rimmed eye glasses that she displayed with such confidence. I wanted to tell her the real reason, but I was so embarrassed, and I was afraid that she might try and help by calling my parents. What a disaster that would be, I thought. In hindsight, it may have been an opportunity for help. That being said, if there is a teenager reading this story, learn from mine, and speak out to a teacher that you like and can trust to have your back. Today, there is much more awareness of domestic violence, and some schools are educated and equipped to help children that speak out. You must speak out. There may be a teacher that can help guide you by seeing the situation and offering different options to take in order to make things better. When I was a child, speaking out to me meant someone calling home. And someone calling home meant a beating. What if I was not thinking so much of an outcome? What if I had just spoken out and trusted life a little more? Many schools in the United States today are aware of domestic violence and are much more open to inquire about situations in the home. They are not educated, however, on the subject and so it is up to the abused to speak out and communicate this for the safety and mental hygiene of yourself, and others. If you are a teacher reading this story, follow your intuition. If you sense there is some hidden situation that is underlying, don't be afraid to ask. It is not probing if your heart is in the right place. It is not meddling if your only intent is to help the student. Put yourself in the shoes of the child for a moment, and try to remember how timid and impressionable you were at that age. Instead of direct questioning, perhaps you could tell the student a story and see if it resonates with them? And if it does, in that moment see where that leads to, in helping. Teachers can be like mentors that are much needed to assist preteens and teens growing up.

One day, my father decided to put the family television out to the curb. He judged that it was all rubbish, and it took us away from our chores and homework. He was convinced that it was bad for the mind. Looking back, he was probably right. We didn't have a television for a few years. I may have been in the seventh or eighth grade. The social studies teacher gave the class an assignment that required us to watch *"Roots"* on the television, and write a paper on it using the outlines he had given to us. It was a TV miniseries that was based on Alex Haley's 1976 novel, *"Roots: The Saga of an American Family"*. This assignment counted as a very large portion of our quarterly grade. The day it was due,

I was the only student that had no papers to hand in. The teacher collected all the papers from everyone except me. We had been seated alphabetically, and so my desk was way in the back of the classroom. He stood up and looked over the others toward me while we all sat at our desks, and asked aloud, "Miss Sanders. Where is your assignment?" I was speechless. Everyone turned their heads back towards me. They all gazed at me with curiosity. The classroom was so quiet that you could hear a pin drop. He remained standing at his desk, shooting out daggers at me with his eyes. He was one of my first male teachers, with a very hard edge, and I was feeling so threatened by that fact alone. Given my environment at home, the only action I was accustomed to taking was to freeze. He continued, "I don't have to remind you that failing to hand it in will affect your grade tremendously, do I?" He continued a public display of verbal badgering, while all I could hear inside this dark cloud around him was a distant, distorted, and blurry background of his voice in slow motion telling me how disappointed he was because he believed me to be a smart student. The voice came from behind the thickness of the air that I could barely breathe in. My eyes hopped to the right and then left, as I looked around at all of the faces. Thirty-four eyeballs from all directions staring at me. My focus caught up with the teacher's tall and upright stance through the distance of the suffocating classroom. Finally, I blurted out in response, "I don't have a television at home". He looked at me wide eyed in amazement. At first, I could sense that he didn't even believe me. I imagined that he judged my response was meant as a joke. It was as if he felt I was mocking him. Immediately, I crawled inside my head. Was this adult I titled as a teacher actually that full of ego that he was compelled to make this all about him? Yes. His mocking tone replied, "You don't have a TV?" "No", I said. There were sounds of chuckling in the air. The laughter actually made the air lighter, although I knew they were all laughing at me. I watched everyone and observed. Most of the students laughed out loud. Some students laughed with a little less outward expression, but I felt their breaths of laughter sweep over the back of my neck from behind. Others laughed as if they were expected to laugh, perhaps by the cool kids or bullies. I will never know. I looked over to my friend. She was not laughing. She returned my look and then looked down. I felt her compassion. She knew the truth. She didn't have the courage to stand up for me, but she didn't laugh. And so for that, I was honored with her respect, her validation, and her love. The amount of time I took to observe others around the classroom felt like forever on the hands of the clock, but it was just a few moments that had gone by. I was trying not to cry, and I remember feeling the tremendous heat coming out of my red face, as the blood pulsated my neck and chest. I could hear my heart beating in my ear drums. I held my weighted chin up. The teacher stared into my water filled eyes. He then quieted the students in the room and resumed class.

Much later in life, I discovered that I was gifted with an acute sense of discernment. It has become a valuable tool in my conscious years. This is a coaching moment for teachers, however. If there is a teacher reading this story that comes across a similar experience with a student in his or her classroom, it is always best to approach the situation without the ego. That means you will not let your thinking mind attach feelings onto your thoughts, which are illusory anyway, and put your full focus and attention on the present moment. You may ask yourself, is this a good time to address the student? You may be surprised to hear the answer is an astounding no. After addressing the student privately, always choose to use your senses, instead of a predetermined judgment on the situation. What are you hearing, and seeing, but more importantly, where are you looking? Are you seeing into the heart? What is your inner voice telling you? Get a sense of this before you think and talk. Sometimes to be a masterful teacher, it is required to see a student's heart. If you are given the choice to humiliate or elevate a student, always choose the latter. We need teachers to show dignity and respect to children of all ages across the globe. When you make a student feel ashamed and foolish by injuring their dignity and self-respect, especially publicly, you add more pain and invite potential suffering onto a person who you really know nothing about. It is not your responsibility to know the ins and outs of a student's life, however, as a human being, it is your responsibility to express love and kindness. In doing this, it means acknowledging your students. Elevating even the smallest accomplishments. Honoring their very existence. If teachers could master a path of love, they could master a path of mentorship. After all, isn't a teacher a mentor?

One day when I was about eleven years of age, one of

my brothers came home with a broken or sprained ankle from an injury he suffered from a school sport. My father acted out in a terrible rage. This accident was how he justified his rules and rationalized his anger. He threw my brother into the wrought iron banister which slit the corner of his eye. I remember being on the top of the staircase crying. I was so scared that my brother's eye would have permanent damage. It was traumatizing. He made my brother mend the wall that was now broken. That was the first and only time I heard my father curse. I recall wanting my father to simply put my brother in the car and take him to a hospital to have the foot and eye looked after. Instead, he chose to use this event as a way to prove why he had the rules that he had, and express his disappointment through violence. Children need affection from their parents, and they need to feel loved and safe. When the pressure is high, children would benefit if their parents could use those heightened opportunities to practice patience, love, and compassion. If they could learn to stay present, their actions would come from a conscious state where the mind and heart can connect. Alternatively, anger acting out in violence is the unconscious choice that will harm children inwardly and outwardly every time.

You, as the reader may judge this action of my father's as insane. That moment in time was exactly that. Insanity. If you are a parent reading this book, I ask that you view your own parental experiences and consider how your reactions today can be applied differently. Have you ever gotten angry and even out of control when your child got hurt while disobeying a rule? You may not have thrown or further injured your child physically, but have you added pain to your child emotionally and mentally with your verbiage? Perhaps you have told your child that they are a disappointment? Maybe you cursed at them, or put them down. You're a loser. You're a failure. You are dead to me. This is why you can never be trusted. I expected more from you, and this is the thanks that I get. You disgust me. You're just like your mother. You're just like your father. You're just like your sister, or brother. I hope that when you grow up, you have a kid just like yourself, as your punishment. Why do you always make my life harder? You have no regard for how hard I work to give you the life that you have. If I didn't have to support you, I wouldn't be here. These examples are all comments that I have personally experienced, and that loved ones in my life have shared with me in their own experience.

So how damaging do you feel words of this nature may be for a child growing up? How deep do you sense these words resonate in your child for years to come? If you took your ego out of the picture and removed the need to be right, and the need to control, and the need to show your emotions from the experience, then what is left? What is left is a more conscious parent who is able to take a more mindful action. Perhaps you will put a punishment in place without the added drama. And once this is done, maybe the child or teenager acts out in anger from the punishment and the teenager's ego pushes your buttons all over again. Then what? Walk away. Let the child finish his or her dramatic display but do nothing. Reacting to your child's tantrum will only spin you into the temporary insanity yourself. Keep your inner peace and stay in a state of love. The ego cannot feed on peace and love. It can only feed on pain. Eventually, the anger stops when it has nothing else to feed off of. You can always return afterward to address what it all meant if needed. But reacting to the anger while it's alive will spiral into unconscious actions that come from the depths of hell. Choose wisely and walk away. I speak from my own experience as a child, and as a parent.

All of the college degrees in the world cannot teach you experience. The trick is to become present in every moment. Take notes as you walk through each experience, and refer to them in the next one so that the mistakes become lesser and lesser. Situations may not always turn perfect, but the choice to have peace in situations is always there. And if you have peace in a situation, then it truly is perfect.

What I found is that many parents have an addiction to being right. This addiction bleeds into your child, and it won't be long before your child has adopted those same behaviors and belief systems. On the other hand, it can also be deeply embedded as a belief system in your child growing up, that he or she is, in fact, always wrong. This leaves them believing that they are inadequate, undeserving, and unworthy. The child may grow up timid, fearful, and insecure. This can lead to their own secret addictions to alcohol, drugs, sex, anorexia, cutting, and things of that nature. Either result does not serve the child's true purpose or true nature. Either result demonstrates just how insane the need to be right is.

Remembrance of Love

Let us fast forward at this moment, for the sake of this lesson on needing to be right, and tie it back to the importance and weight this has on raising children with love. It was 1992, and I walked into a book store downtown in Greenwich Village, Manhattan. I was clearly searching for something in my adult life. I was feeling unhappy, and couldn't put my finger on why this was so. There were questions I had and some pieces to this mysterious puzzle to life were missing. I was in a loving relationship with a British man, who I also considered my best friend. My decisions at that particular time were unconscious, and so I based them on everything that people in my life considered was right and safe. None of it panned out to feel right, and all of it kept me in a safety net I will call fear, because it diminished everything that I loved, including myself. Circumstances left me feeling unfulfilled, unimportant, misunderstood, and unsupported in my dreams and visions. This is because I was looking outward for self-fulfillment. My visions and his were miles apart. The obscurity of it all left me feeling powerless. The spark in me seemed dead, because the things I loved and the things that I resonated with deep down, I could no longer see and appreciate. It was as though I could only hear the sounds of invisible waters.

So there I was, in this quaint old book store, searching through the aged and musty smelling wooden book shelves for answers to my soul. I pulled out a spiritual book whose title caught my attention. Gallivanting across the creaking floor toward the back of the shop, I sat on a worn sofa that I spotted way back in the corner. The sofa smelled like it was there since pre-war and indeed, it dominated the air around me. I began to thumb through some pages and walked over toward the front of the store. I bought the book and returned back to that same neighborhood book shop and purchased the same author's cassette tapes so I could have some guided meditation for relaxation. Her cassette tapes became a doorway into the beginning of my awakening, although I did not know this at the time. Her guided meditation always suggested that the past has no power over me. The affirmations were spoken in the present tense. This was my first introduction to meditation and affirmations. Little did I know that this earlier experience was to become a daily part of my life today. I remember she asked a question in one of the meditational tapes, as she referenced it to 'A Course in

Miracles'. She asked something like this: *"Is it better to be right, or is it better to be loved?"* I pondered that question. The content of the cassette tapes brought me to a journey back into my memories of growing up. She talked a lot about the inner child. This language was foreign to me. My inner what? It was at this time, I imagined that my childhood was all behind me, but I realized it wasn't behind me at all. Rather I was blocking years of mental, emotional and physical abuse that was resurfacing as the dreams of being a dancer and actress had been on the back burner for no other reasons except me buying into other people's reasons, and their need to be right. When I later went back to studying acting and performing in Manhattan, these suppressed pains worked great for me as I became a Stanislavsky method actor, because I had lots to draw from. But that wasn't a full proof acting method for me when I was performing the same show with the same script every night. Mental recall can drive one mentally nuts, even for the actor. This began my search for an acting method that I could depend on. I wanted something that allowed dialogue to feel fresh and real every time. Finally, I was introduced to Sanford Meisner's method which soon became my 'go to' tool for performing. Later in life, I discovered exactly how mindful and present his method was in its application to life itself. Astounding observation for me, which I will discuss later on in chapters.

This question that rang in my head, *"Is it better to be right, or is it better to be loved?"* needed answers. To me, at surface level, I imagined it suggested that it is better to be loved by someone, then to win a discussion or argument with someone. This is very helpful to remember when experiencing a conflict between two people. Always choose love over winning. I resonated with this. At a much deeper level, however, I see much more in that question. Turning away from ego and holding onto love is important, but this doesn't suggest that you are to become a victim of someone's ego and pain. It took me decades to stop aiming towards making other people right so that they would love me. If you feel the need to stop being true to yourself in order to get love from another, then you have not learned love. Stop looking to the world for love. Anything and anyone the world can give you is short lived. You were given the Divine gift of love within, which far exceeds any temporary pleasures that the external world can bring. This Divine love is infinite. This Divine love is eternal. No one and no experience has the power to take it away. It is your free gift. It is locked in a safe within your heart but you have the key. No one else holds the key to your heart but you. As you open it, you will dwell in the realm of where true joy resides. This joy is triumph. To find triumph is to have found success. It is to have found the one thing that truly matters. Because the truth is, success is not a destination you arrive at or a title that you achieve. You don't arrive at it because you already have it. Success is inherent. It is an immanent attribute that dwells deep within. It's there. You just need to find it. And to find it is to have found the secret to success. The secret to success is discovering love, not from another person or thing, rather within one's self. Knowing that it is not something outside in the world, but is something that is within. This knowing is the internal bridge that takes you out of suffering and into peace. This knowing pulls you through the gap. It is your remembrance of love.

This love is your light. It is for you to glow, and to shine onto others. Until we have this love for self, we cannot experience love elsewhere. Don't seek it in others. Instead, share it with others. Your soul is nourished by what you share, not by what you receive. So be the living expression of your higher-self, your inner-child, and this love and light. Honor this living expression of love, by disallowing experience and people to put your light under a rock. Your light is your gift and is purposed to ignite others so that those who are smoldering can be lit again. This is why we are here. There is a passion within you that keeps that flame alive, and if that passion is forgotten it dies out. Live your passion. If you forgot what that passion was, find it. Find your treasure. Encourage others to find theirs. Try not to meddle in people's lives by offering your opinions on what you believe they should do with their life. Their heart will guide them. We are not here to tell people what to do. We are here to love. We are only here to love. And as we love, we support. Support holds up, assists, and approves. Support does not demand, order, or instruct. Even as a parent, we are to love and support our children. When they are infants we must lift them, and hold them, and nurture them, and love on them constantly. Stop leaving your infant child to scream itself to sleep in a crib that has no heart beat or vibration. Infant babies require love and affection. They cannot survive this human life without it. Stop trying to train an infant, and start loving it.

'In the United States, 1944, an experiment was conducted on forty newborn infants to determine whether humans could thrive alone on basic physiological needs without affection. Twenty newborn infants were housed in a special facility where they had caregivers who would go in to feed them, bathe them and change their diapers, but they would do nothing else. The caregivers had been instructed not to look at or touch the babies more than what was necessary, never communicating with them. All their physical needs were attended to scrupulously and the environment was kept sterile, none of the babies becoming ill. The experiment was halted after four months, by which time, at least half of the babies had died at that point. At least two more died even after being rescued and brought into a more natural familial environment. There was no physiological cause for the babies' deaths; they were all physically very healthy. Before each baby died, there was a period where they would stop verbalizing and trying to engage with their caregivers, generally, stop moving, and neither cry or change expression. Death would follow shortly. The babies who had "given up" before being rescued, died in the same manner, even though they had been removed from the experimental conditions.

The conclusion was that nurturing is actually a very vital need in humans.'

This is so disturbing on so many levels. Has society come to this? Do we need to learn about past experiments and create more in order to understand that love is the heartbeat of life? Has this world become this mad? Yes. I could barely write about this experiment without tears rolling down my eyes. When will we wake up and take a conscious shift? When will we wake up and choose to love? It begins with all of us, individually in order to see a collective shift. The need to love and be loved never ends. Love one another. This is God's heart.

All my life I struggled to find this hole in my heart. Why did I have to seek answers about love in books? My parents didn't teach me, my marriages didn't show me, and my divorces nearly killed me. I wrote this book to show you how experience taught me love and can do the same for you. Experience brought me to my heart center. Experience came to me like a double edged sword, though. One side cut me like a knife, repeatedly. While the other side carved right into me, exposing my very essence. I encourage you today, to find the masterpiece that is within you. Be the sculptor of your own life. Don't let others chisel away at you, and don't chisel away at others.

Know that you came into this world by purpose. You are not random. No thing in life is random. Every bit that you are made up of is unique and special and has its purpose in the Universe. If you are a parent or a care giver, know that the same is true of your children. Tell them this with confidence, as often as you can. Love them and assist them in developing this capacity to love for generational blessings. It is why we are here. As parents, when our children are babies learning to walk we help them along by holding them up. We allow them to bear most of their weight on us as they muster up the courage to take those steps on their own. If there is a physical situation that requires attention, you give them crutches or braces and help them learn how to maneuver and adapt with them. You don't sit there idle while pointing at them and ordering them as to where and how you believe they are to walk, do you? The point is that you are not here to command, dictate, mandate and require how, when and where the child must walk. You are there to express love, and be their parental pillars that can support, under-gird, and reinforce the matters of their heart as they experience each moment and grow in life. Love is not taught with language. Love is taught through experience. It is always nice to say that we love someone but it is essential that we express love in all that we do so that love can be experienced. Give your child a love experience. Disconnect from the perception manipulation that you have undergone in your own past upbringing so that you don't put it on your child. Stop pressing upon what your ego mind believes and start to support your child and loved ones with the individuated acceptance of what is. This is how to break the mold for generational blessings.

When you start enforcing belief systems on yourself and others, you take on identities and put yourself and them in prison. What I learned from personal life experiences, some which I share on these pages is that we need to disconnect ourselves from this skewed environment of power and control, and fundamentally disconnect ourselves from the massive influence that our brain has on human perception and reality. Why? Because we are all consciousness. We are all love. This body is a vehicle and needs to be driven by the heart.

What happens when you choose to be driven by thoughts in the mind? What about the desires in your thoughts that run your life, convincing you that until you have them, you cannot be happy? What does your internal dialogue sound like? You cannot be happy until you get the promotion. You cannot be happy until you own the company. You cannot be happy until you are married. You cannot be happy until you have a child. You cannot be happy until you get that mortgage and live in the house of your dreams. You cannot be happy until you pay off that mortgage. You cannot be happy unless the courts award you custody of the children. You cannot be happy unless you have been validated by every person in life that you demand attention and acceptance from. Does any of this sound familiar?

Thoughts will sabotage you. Let these thoughts go and remember that the mind can be a blessing or a curse. It can be a wonderful servant or a terrible master. When we let go of desire and thought, the identification of desirous thoughts, there will be a sense of freedom. Peace. After all, our natural being is to be without need. This is true peace. I believe we are truly rich when we want for nothing. Even from God. Because at this point in life, after experiencing a few disasters, I have come to the realization that nothing is forever, and everything is for a while. This is truth. This is freedom. Knowing this gives you the power back to the only thing that is real. And the only thing that is real, is the present moment. Knowing this allows you to live in love, and not fear. These are your only two choices. When you can let go of the mental noise and conditioned mind patterns that have been running your life, you can begin to release all hindrance or restraints that have been stopping you from embracing the true reflection of life itself. Life itself is love, not want. Life itself is being, not waiting to become. Life itself can only be now.

Instead of focusing solely on the thinking mind, begin to put your attention within. Focus on the soul. Shut off the chatter in the mind, and just listen. Practice this by simple meditation. It need not be complicated. Don't order, wish, complain, or beg for things. Rather get still, focus on the breath, and listen to what your heart is trying to tell you. This is meditation. It is being still in your mind. It is part of every tradition in the world. It has nothing to do with religion, belief, idolatry or doctrine. Many confuse and compare this with prayer. There is a difference between prayer and meditation. Prayer is your speaking to God. Meditation is allowing God to speak to you. But it speaks in silence. And it is in that silence where it begins to manifest into inspiration and intuition. Prayer focuses outward, where meditation is an inward focus. Many people are led to believe that meditation is to be done a certain way, with a set of rules, and with a specific result in mind to be gained. In truth, meditation is not an act of doing, rather it is a state of being. We can all meditate anywhere, and at any time. It is to be still without thought. And in that stillness, we can be raised or transported above it all. Above all of the madness, that collective unconsciousness has manifested on this earth. Because at soul level there is pure consciousness. There is that connection with Oneness and that alert awareness in the heart that puts things back in spiritual order. Remember, you are truly a spiritual being having a human experience. Not the other way around.

I skewed off course a bit, in order to stress how important is to understand that the remembrance of love has everything to do with understanding and letting go of your personal upbringing, raising your own children, and taking the individual conscious shift needed for generational blessings. I couldn't be more passionate about driving this home. Having said that, let us move on to a few more childhood experiences.

The Witch under Water

We crawled on our hands and knees in a plastic tube, shaped in the form of a maze. The maze was immersed in and surrounded by a thick body of water. The only place for oxygen that we knew of, was in this bubble-like tubing. The echoes of the water bounced off the sides of the plastic as we swooshed through the tube without sight beyond it. The plastic tube was white, although it did not light the way. We couldn't see the water, but the awareness was there. There was a sense of vastness in the water surrounding us. At every intersection of the maze, we scattered to the right, and then to the left, never knowing which way was safe. Like tiny ants in combat, we scurried one behind the other. The tubing was barely wide enough or high enough to house more than one body on all fours. When the one in the front of the line crawled left at the intersection, we all crawled left. If the front crawler scrambled right at an intersection, we all scrambled right. The goal was to escape the witch that was not too far behind us, as we heard her shrilling voice get closer and closer towards me and my siblings. I was at the end of the line and closest to the witch. This was my recurring dream as a little girl growing up. It visited many nights per week and went on for years.

Going to sleep was dreadful, and trying to fall back asleep after the upsetting of this nightmare was an even bigger challenge. I don't recall ever telling my parents the dream. I do recall, however, many times well before dawn running into their bedroom and hopping aboard the blanket between my mom and dad. I remember this nightmare vividly and can recall each episode. Only now it does not haunt me. I don't need to be a rocket scientist to know that it was obvious I was feeling afraid in my home growing up, having emotional problems coping with it, and having difficulties resolving it. I found that this is what most PTSD phycologists may even tell you. Although this may be relatively true, it was not absolute truth. I interpret this nightmare today much differently and use it as a teacher.

The body of water that hugged us was not the external unknown outside our home but was the internal formless presence. The plastic tubing appears to be our home, however, it actually represents the costume that we wore growing up. Let us call this costume victim. The witch was not my father, rather, the witch was fear. The action was expressive in its desire to escape fear but as unconscious as the turns we made. The intersections were not choices but were decoys from truth. Because this was my dream, I can tell you that the nuance of it embodied a desperate journey in search for love.

It is interesting to me how I included the siblings in my personal quest to escape fear. I imagined that because we were all in it together, we all had the same fear, the same needs, and the same problem to resolve. Within the dream, I chose to follow the path of the ones ahead of me, which never got me anywhere, except at a new intersection for tomorrow night's sequel. I imagine if I were conscious enough to envision myself outside of the maze, I may have discovered at an earlier age that I could pierce through the scary plastic encasement and swim to uncertainty, leaving the witch to drown in her own environment. I could have done this if I saw myself as one with the water...the internal formless presence. I would have glided beneath the ocean's surface, and battling the ripples atop would no longer drown me. The ever changing waves of impermanence on the surface can be understood as relative, but not absolute. Just as one wave ends a new one begins. There is nothing solid about it. In fact, it is completely unsustainable. Because of this, it is not absolute. The only thing that is absolute is this moment. And at this moment, there is undoubtedly an opportunity to experience the infinite and formless ocean so to speak, that can only be described as presence. This is my metaphorical description of the difference between the form and the formless. The external world, and internal presence. When we come to this point in life where we can connect both, there is opportunity for wisdom to enter, and mindful actions to be taken. When you can see, breathe, and live life beneath all of the layers of the external world, which I will call labels and life situations, then you will know what actions to take in the external world, because the answers are coming from a present, highly acute state of awareness that tells you, okay, this situation may be relatively true but it is not absolute. What do I mean by that? Well, the current situation is never permanent, just as the waves are ever changing on the ocean's surface. The only thing that is real is the present moment. The present moment does not lie behind or ahead. It is as it is. And so in this moment of acceptance to what is, you can choose to release yourself from the suffering in a situation. In that knowing, the right choice will be made because it will be the conscious choice. I beat myself up for a few years wondering why I made bad choices in relationships. But the truth is, I was not conscious during those years and so, I kept manifesting that which my mind was already conditioned to knowing. If I were conscious, I would have been able to see clearly and make fruitful choices. What I found is that we tend to stay stagnant when we are uncertain, but the truth is that we can never really be certain of any outcome. Instead, know that there is great wisdom in uncertainty. I heard this from many spiritual leaders in the past years and it wound up being some of the best advice I had come across, especially when it comes to releasing fear in one's life. Use challenges as opportunities for growth and make conscious choices for change. Don't get caught up in the mental drama of it all. See the waves, but don't dwell there. Be in the calm of the ocean. Most of us walk around reacting to every life situation unconsciously and then blame everyone and every circumstance for our suffering. We chose our suffering from dwelling on the story that we add onto what has happened.

So how can you change this? Stop thinking, and start feeling. You can only feel what is at this moment. You cannot feel something that has come and gone. Don't dwell behind you. Dwelling on something that has already happened is buying into what the thinking mind, which is always the ego, is telling you. Stop concentrating so much on your future, as it can be a recipe for fear. You must feel from this instant, or you will not transcend the suffering. If you always focus on what is wrong, or that which does not express love, you will never emerge from it. The goal, my dear readers, is to transcend. Be in this moment with clear vision.

And in this moment is where miracles begin to happen. Remember, the goal is always to transcend. In the Book of Matthew in the Bible, three days after the crucifixion of Jesus, it reads, *"He is not here. He has risen."* This is a beautiful story of transcendence. He manifested glory in His darkest hour. It shows the powerful transformation of a spiritual being in its human experience. You can honor the cross and what it represents, but focus on how Jesus transcended it all. It is always the miracle of rising out of the darkness that matters. It sends a powerful message of how we can all rise from whatever the external world brings us when we live our truth in the light. So don't dwell in the past. Stop focusing on someone or something that was there, when you are here. Be open to all of the glory the present moment has to offer. Instead of manifesting what your unconscious ego has convinced you of as your fate, manifest love and peace in your life today. And for today, let go of all guilt or regret for the choices you've made in the past. Just as you should not dwell behind you, you shouldn't dwell on your mistakes either. The truth is that you have made no mistakes. Every choice you have made is the exact choice you needed to make in order to get you to where you are now. I reiterate this throughout these pages so that the only thing you need to get to is the present moment.

When I was that child living in a domestically violent home, of course, the pain was to be inevitable. How could it not be? As I grew older in years, I harbored the pain, which was also inevitable. We all suppress past pain in different degrees. None of us are free from pain. Pain, however, is not our enemy. Pain is our natural path to enlightenment. When life as you knew it has suddenly dissolved, there is an amazing portal that begins to open. Should you choose to enter, will determine if and when you evolve. Conversely, if you do not learn how to transmute pain into enlightenment, it can spiral downward into intense suffering. What blocks us from this spiritual transmutation and inner self-growth is the unwillingness to let go of the added, unhappy story. When we hold onto the added unhappy story, we hold onto ego. That holding on allows ego to take over, and the only thing gained from all of it is suffering. This took me decades to learn.

Looking at the nightmare with the witch under water now, I realize that the very thing that kept me running within the walls of that tube was the very thing I was trying to escape. Fear. Fear of what, you might ask? Fear of injury? Risk? Not being protected? Maybe death? All of it. There is no safety in fear, however. Safety is not found behind walls, although fear will tell you it is. Fear will actually convince you that it wants to keep you safe. This is a lie. Love tells you that you are already safe. There is no risk or danger with love. Love cannot die because it is as eternal and formless as the galaxies above and beyond. So I encourage you to turn from fear and stop believing it. I will discuss this in more detail, later in chapters. For now, read on about a young girl's precocious walk into lion's den.

The Lion's Den

I remember one day my father was so angry with me. I hadn't a clue what set him off. I judged his anger as unwarranted. What I did know was that his dictatorship set the mood in the house, as it always did. It was the all too familiar silence before the storm. Since I was the one being punished, I was not permitted to hide in my bedroom. I had to stay in the kitchen with my sniffling mother, which came with an entirely different set of emotions, not far from his sight or hearing. My father was in the living room sitting on the couch for hours, in complete silence. This was typical behavior for him when this character came to visit. His need to control and be justified for his anger compelled my mother to whisper to me in the kitchen a request that was something like this; "Go in there and tell your father you're sorry." I looked at my mother as the red heat began to climb from the bottom of my toes to the crown of my head. Perplexed with the internal wonder of how anyone would even suggest such a thing, I didn't see how an apology could assist in lifting the silent fog that filled our home. All I could hear in my thinking mind was how I was being pushed into lion's den. I sought solace as I looked into her empty eyes that conveyed no signs of concrete answers to peace. It seemed to me that her only hope was that if this worked, we would all have a better afternoon. So, reluctantly I went in.

      With terror in my eyes, I began to walk slowly into the living room where the lion was. One very slow step at a time. Left. Then right. My entire body trembled as I put one foot in front of me, and then the next. The floor beneath the carpet creaked at every step as urine began to trickle down the inside of my left leg. Finally, I stopped about six feet from him, as he sat on the sofa with both of his eyes closed. Like an eagle, he opened one eye and then the other as he gazed over at me. My lips curved downward in the opposite direction of a smile and began to quiver. A breath, and then, "I'm sorry daddy." My father commanded, "Come here." Frozen in my tracks, I stood there. I couldn't move. He gazed at me longer. After what seemed like an eternity he finally he said, "Never fear man. The only one you should fear is God." At that moment all I could think inside my head was what a bunch of baloney that was. What did that even mean? What kind of distorted, skewed statement of sorts was that? As it turned out, this plan to enter the lion's den did not result in the ending hoped for. For me, it was traumatic. The internal pain was real, as it latched onto the thoughts in my head, resulting in my pain from the absence of love, nonacceptance, and an undeniable void of compassion. I remember that day as if the hands of the clock stopped for forty some odd years. I was about nine or ten years of age. I remember the anger I felt with my mother, although it was short-lived. It amazed me that she could be married to someone for nearly twenty-five years, have four children together in such a dysfunctional violent environment, and not know that saying sorry, would not be enough to slow down a mentally unstable man that was already on an express locomotion to insanity. I imagine that his own suppressed inner pain from past experiences had taken over and consumed him. When we use the expression, he was out of his mind, it means exactly that. No one in their conscious mind will behave this way. It is an unconscious mind that drives someone to act out in such a manner. So, they actually are out of their mind. They almost cannot even be judged, because the internal dialogue in their mind runs the show. It is like moments of pure insanity.

As my memory serves me, my mom spent most of these times in the kitchen. I couldn't begin to guess what was going on inside her mentally or emotionally, but the external memory I had of her was always sniffling with rolled up tissues tucked into her pants, skirt, apron, or in her nostril. My mother did a lot of silent dish washing and in my view, nonsensical busy work in the kitchen. It always seemed to me that it was where she escaped from the environment around us. Perhaps it was the only way she could deal with it all, tune out, and pray. I saw her as the quiet mouse in the house that lost her voice. After all, she walked on egg shells with the rest of us.

There was a time, however, that I remember my mother defending us kids. I remember it very well. My father was on a horrific war path, and we were all getting beat. We each had to wait our turn...again in the living room. I grew to hate that living room. My mother could not bear it any longer and shouted out tearfully as she approached him. "That's enough!" she cried out. My father then went to push and strike her. In turn, both my brothers jumped on my father, to protect my mother. That evolved into insane madness, and then ended in a lot of tears, physical and emotional pain, and utter weariness. My father felt as if my brothers ambushed him. It was, however, the first time I felt united as an army. I know that sounds crazy but I have no other way of wording the feeling that overcame me. It wasn't long after that awful episode that my parents were to divorce.

Death in Life's Clothing

My mother's cousin came over one day and said we were going to have a family meeting in my parent's bedroom. I don't remember where my father was at the time, but he was not in the house. She directed us all to go upstairs for a family meeting, to the same bedroom that I spent endless hours on the floor listening to Cinderella as a little girl. She was the only one that talked, while my mother characteristically sniffled and looked down and away from all of us. My cousin said, "Your mother is suffering." There went that voice in my head again, "She? You mean, we. We are all suffering…a lot." She continued by telling us that our mom needs to divorce our father, but she can't do it without the support of all four children. We all agreed to support her in this action, as scared as my mom was. I felt that was going to be our ticket to freedom. Soon we would all be out of domestic prison. This day, I felt united as a family instead of an army. Sounds crazy, I know. But remember, we were all in survival mode. Fight or flight. So we all seemed to learn how to fly with broken wings. This is how I saw it. Five wounded birds flying out of a cage in different directions to their freedom. The sixth wounded bird was our father who never healed, and experienced his own very real pain, and suffered from it because of his deep identification with his mind's perception of it all. In between the layers of his unconscious moments, however, there were some loving experiences and smiling moments. But not many. I knew it was not his heart that was violent, but his deep seated pain and conditioned mind patterns that ran him into a state of insanity at any given moment.

Having said that, there were moments when my father was very conscious, very alert, and very loving. My father had a heart for humanity. He was a generous and righteous man in so many ways and yet, he struggled with deep pain from his own past. Much later in life, when I began reading spiritual texts, I understood this as pain bodies. What are pain bodies? Layers of negative emotional charge that accumulate, and are stored inside our bodies. These layers prevent us from experiencing peace and over all well-being. It seemed to me that his old emotional pain is what put him in a state of unconsciousness every time triggered. The stories I shared are not to put my father in a bad light. I loved my father deeply and this love I have for him was no secret. While writing this book, my father died. He took sudden physical illness and died within what seemed to be about ten to fourteen days. It was said that he died of natural causes. Physically that was the case. But emotionally and mentally, the flame inside of him died a long time ago. That, for me, was the real tragedy. I have experienced this internal death twice, during my own life, and can tell you that it is very real and cataclysmic at its core. When something dies inside of us while we live, we experience the catastrophic downfall of our very essence. As the spirit in you dies, your mortal self loses reason to exist. When I reached this point, twice, which I will share in the next few chapters, I just wanted to cross the great divide, and slip away into nothingness. It seemed less painful. The truth is, I already had slipped away. It is like living death in life's clothing. So I understood how my beloved father felt deep down. I had great compassion for him.

About a year before his death, I had a conversation with my father by telephone. The course of our conversation led me to believe that he was suffering a severe depression. I knew that he felt the identity of what he attached himself to in the past, had gone away. I asked him if he wanted to die. He said he did. He talked about going home to the Lord. At that time, I sent a text to a sibling of mine, who returned a text back to me. It read about how sad it is that he will die of a broken heart. The text spoke volumes. I believed that to be a possibility. It was as if his once hopeful heart was damaged. It was no longer in one piece or in working order. He had given up all hope of repairing his broken heart, and all hope for loneliness to dissipate. I could hear the despair and hurt in his voice. He was actually angry. Although he made peace with most of us, he never seemed to be fully at peace. Although our father was a God loving man, my feeling is that he was challenged with the concept of letting go of the past, and the rights and wrongs of it, and forgiveness of himself and others. He seemed to be a tortured soul, never really finding his way back home. Having deep conversations in the past with my father, it was evident that he was a man who talked to God daily. It was also evident, only after he died, that he loved us all, dearly. He marveled at the beauty of us children and cherished every photograph that he had of us from birth to adulthood. He was tormented by the conflicts of the past we experienced together. He was also tormented with his addiction to be in control, and his addiction to be right. Addiction to being right and non-forgiveness are epidemics in the world today. Why would anyone choose to be addicted to the two things that create division and disease?

I imagine that he struggled with forgiving himself, as well as a few others that in speculation may have been a turning point or opportunity for his rising into truth and the power that the present moment had to offer him. The repair, however, needed to be internal, at the core of where hurt and betrayal are harbored and where the unhappy stories start lining up. Not addressing this at its core kept non-forgiveness at the fore front of his battle field. Having had much pain from his past as a child born during the great depression, a soldier on the front lines in the Korean War, and as a husband and father who couldn't escape his own pain, I had deep compassion for him. I felt his pain.

Fifteen months later he was to die from a massive stroke and heart attack. This was the ten day period before his death. During this time, just after his second stroke, which left him without speech, I spoke to him by telephone. Living nearly sixteen hundred miles away, the only thing that seemed to matter was the moment at hand, and immediate verbal communication was what I chose. I called the hospital several times, until I could communicate with a nurse in the hospital unit where my father was being cared for, that I needed her assistance in the phone call and that it was important to me, and ultimately, him. He was in a vegetative state, and so the nurse thought it was senseless, but none the less, she agreed to do it. As the nurse held the phone to my father's ear, I greeted him. I said, "Hi daddy, it's me. Lily." He let out a moan and I could hear his breathing. I knew he had woken from his vegetative state in that moment. I told him how much we all love him, and that everyone has forgiven him. I told him that if he wanted to let go, it's okay. I told him not to be afraid. He began breathing even louder. I knew he heard me. "I love you daddy" I cried out. "Do you love me?" I asked. "O ya" he responded back loudly. I cried. I had already forgiven him and set him free from my mind, and had also released any old pain that was there. But I felt it may help him let go of his own pain if he knew this. My hope was that he would forgive himself. The nurse came in and I heard her call him by name, "You're awake?" and then she hung up the phone. Apparently, she had the phone resting beside his ear the entire time as she checked on other patients. Five days later he died. The heart of this story is that we siblings united as a force of love, and not an army, to honor my father's life in his death. I gave a eulogy that celebrated his life, and the happy moments and memories that he brought us in our life. There was heartfelt tears that were shed and even a few moments of laughter as I spoke of only funny memories. There was a beautiful comedic quality about my father, and it was refreshing to re-live that, even if for a moment, at the funeral service as his body was lying in the coffin behind me.

The Eulogy

"Today we celebrate our father's life. Not his death.
In this life, he was a son, a brother, a soldier, a husband, a father, and a stress analyst.
To me, he was my dad.
Our father had intense love for three things. God, his family, and humanity. What sets him apart from most was his innate gift to befriend anyone and everyone that needed a friend.

It was quite typical for my dad to invite someone we hardly knew to dinner after church on Sunday...One of those invites became part of the family temporarily as we moved a Hindu from Bombay, India into our home. That's our Dad.

My dad was fond of farming, so we were the only ones in a suburban town that had chickens, a rooster, a guinea pig, a rabbit who I named Lizzie, and oh....a goose egg that we brought home from the farm in Dix Hills, and hatched it under our hen who we named All Spice. The goose was really sweet when it was a gosling, then it soon turned into a huge goose who we named Pronto that would always run after every one of our friends that attempted to walk through the gate of our front yard. So growing up as a teenager, friends would randomly run through our front door without knocking because Pronto was so fast and furious and if he got you in the butt...he really hurt! In fact just recently, about 2 years ago, I ran into an old friend randomly from the old neighborhood and he proceeded to ask, "Remember that goose?"

We also had a parrot named Pee Wee. He loved my father. One day Pee Wee flew out the front door and was gone for hours. My mom and some of us kids were calling his name all around the property. When my dad returned home, he walked about and spotted Pee Wee perched up on a very tall tree behind the bank parking lot next to our house. He looked up and said, "Pee Wee. Come down here. " And Pee Wee flew down to his shoulder immediately. That's my Dad.

My dad was very present in his mother's life, and his siblings and their families. My fondest memories were all of us on Sunday's in Brooklyn with cousins and Aunts and Uncles...and also in New Jersey with other family. He was everyone's, Uncle Mario.

My dad was fond of baking and gardening. I remember how much he used to make homemade Sicilian pizza pies and top them with all of the fresh ingredients from our garden, from the tomatoes to the basil and oregano.

My fondest memory of all is the most recent when he spent time with me and my son in 2005. It was an intangible experience that is incapable of being perceived by the sense of touch but was well received by the heart. Watching him talk to Andrew about things, and answering Andrew's curious questions...to the similarly simple things like cooking a roasted chicken in the oven with my father and seeing most of my siblings come over and enjoy dinner and conversation in my home with his grandchildren was an astonishing event for the Sanders' family. It was a beautiful moment in time.

Because of my father's love for healthy food, my son and I laughed at my Dad as he would stand in our kitchen eating raw broccoli saying, "Mmmmm...tastes just like candy!" That's my Dad.

My father's favorite color was red because it represented the blood of Christ, and white because it represented the light...God. He always wore these colors, even to funerals, and so in his memory, I am following suit, in celebration of his life with all of us. I believe that our father is in his next life now, looking upon all of us with clarity, understanding, and intense love for all."

"Love is not prejudiced and is for all of humanity waiting to be found under every stone unturned."

~Lily Sanders

CHAPTER 3

Generational Blessings

MY FATHER WAS THE MOST INTENSE person I have ever known and his intensity goes on to live in all of us at different degrees. For me, these are fervent years where my awakening has opened a path, so ardent and so consumed by love and compassion for those who are ready to let go of their suffering. For anyone who has been battered or is a batterer and are reading this book, you may already be aware that the after effects from it can turn up in life again and again in some form, whether it's in your own marriage, relationships, and so on. It doesn't necessarily show up in the form of violence either. It can surface itself in other forms, like alcoholism, addictions to prescription drugs or illegal drugs, addictions to power and control, addictions to being right, addictions to sex, high degrees of confrontational characteristics, depression, complete lack of focus and drive, self-deprivation like anorexia, and cutting to name a few. For me, it revived in my life in the form of anorexia, in my earlier years from seventeen years of age until twenty-three years of age. After I released that emotional pain and physical dysfunction, the pain resurfaced with a different face decades later, as I found myself in two marriages that were both laden with different faces of domestic violence. It seemed that I required two tall buildings to fall on my head in order to have an awakening. As comical as this sounds, for some, that is what it takes. When you can no longer stand the suffering in your life, you will make one of two decisions. Take the shift at that moment, or go on suffering until you die or are killed.

This moment is all there is. I urge every reader of this book, to understand that there is no end of the tunnel. The time is now. Stop waiting your entire life for it to begin. Stop looking and waiting for a light at the end of the tunnel, rather seek that light in your heart today. Purpose your now to reignite your spirit and love yourself. Stop believing your thoughts of fear and start seeing your reality as love in the here and now. This message is not new. Spiritual messages never are, because it has been the same message forever and ever. What you need to know, perhaps has been said again and again. The truth is, you have always known this. You just haven't awakened to it yet. Sometimes there are glimpses of this awareness, and then it goes unrecognized again until you are ready to take the conscious shift. Be inspired to unfold truth into your life, where only love exists. It is our free gift and love is not prejudiced. If you have lost the ability to love or feel love, then you will need to re-wire and return to love. How do you do this? Go to the root, and pull it out. For me, this meant facing my own pain, then transmuting it into peace. I was never really certain how to do that effectively. I knew that to dwell on the past was certainly not productive, but I also knew that the corrosion there would kill me if I didn't remove it. Pain seemed to be the root I was looking for. Once I became aware that it was there, I was able to pull the pain from the roots and remove it. Almost instantly an odd sense of peace came over me. What I also found is that hidden and unaddressed pain exists in all of us. This realization helped me see what drives others to their own insanity. Knowing that it is not as much the person, as it is their hidden pains who are the perpetrators, allowed me to let go of all self-blame and also all of the rejection that I was feeling. It also opens the door to forgiveness. If you know someone is out of their mind, it becomes a lot easier to let go of any unconscious acts they have committed against you. For me, this was life changing. I was able to release the anger that I was feeling with past experiences, and also able to love myself again. Many times when someone is living in an abusive environment, the victim begins to believe that there is something wrong with them and that they are somehow responsible for the abuse. Much of this belief stems from the constant emotional abuse encountered, where the abuser tries to convince you that you are the crazy one. Often times they succeed. After a while, you begin to believe everything is your fault. It is an insane form of emotional abuse that unfortunately is an all too common experience among victims. Pain bodies are explained as any deep emotional pain that is in your energy field, which directly generates and accumulates pain in your life. It can be old pain that was never fully addressed, and can also be a collection of old and new pain from your life experiences. In some people, it lies dormant and will surface when triggered. In others, it is highly active all the time. Regardless of how active or inactive it is, the goal is to let it go. Once you can release the pain, you can begin to transmute it into peace. Much of what attributed to my personal awakening was absorbing these concepts from a spiritual teacher for whom I am forever grateful. Of course, there were glimpses of awakenings in the late 80's and early 90's, however, I wasn't fully open and ready. The messages are always out there, floating in bottles across the ocean to our feet by the shore. All we need to do is take heed and be willing to let go of the suffering. Suffering comes in all sizes and shapes. It can be someone undergoing depression, experiencing disease, or something as simple and yet equally debilitating as being miserable for no apparent external reason. We all choose our poison. This isn't to say that we ask for it. It means that we choose to dwell on certain thoughts in the mind's perception of reality that is all an illusion. Any thoughts that keep you out of the present moment, are the same thoughts that keep you in the dark. Whatever is stored inwardly needs to be cleaned, where the only thing left is love. Some holistic health practitioners say that pain bodies are stored in cellular memory, while some spiritual gurus say pain is stored at soul level. Interestingly enough, it has also been referred to as its own entity. The point is, everyone agrees that pain bodies exist in all of us.

So how do we find these disguised opportunities for growth, and how do we let go of our pain once recognized? By coming into presence. When you are focused on the present moment, you are forced to face your pain. Much of this pain comes from emotional wounds. This is where healing begins. This is also where enlightenment happens. We cannot divorce the processing of emotional wounds from our spiritual path. One proceeds the other. Conversely, in this process is also where fear may come knocking. Don't let it in. Deny it. No matter what fear tries to tell you, don't believe it. Believing anything that instills fear is to believe an illusion. The only thing that is real is the present moment. So in this moment, face your pain. You must face your pain, in order to transcend it. Time does not heal pain. Presence does. Waiting for years to pass in order to see pain fade, is like expecting the minute hand to grant you memory loss. It just doesn't work that way. Stop waiting on time. The time is now.

Forgiving and understanding that someone has highly active pain in their energy field do not mean that you are to fall victim to their pain, however. Peel off the victim label and run for your life. In a highly volatile situation, you may need to firmly tell someone to back off, or you will have them removed. Those were the exact words I was advised to use by a retired policeman. At one point in my life, I had to do exactly that. I may have had to run for my life, but there was a wonderful gateway that opened and I found my way back to love. When you feel love within, you honor yourself. And when you honor yourself you attract the same honor and respect from others, including your children. If you are a conscious parent, fear will not stop you from protecting your children. Love will always prevail. Self-honor and self-respect are part of the vital love and support we are to give our children. We give this to them through experience. It is not a family code or handbook we give out when they learn to read. Rather it's a way we feel, how we behave, speak, act and react in each experience together. It is a parent's responsibility to show children love, honor, and respect in all that we do so that they can experience it for themselves. If we can do this, one by one, we can change lives. We need to start promoting values as human beings which can be universal regardless of life situations, race, religion, or belief systems. This is how we can manifest and create generational blessings. We are human beings whose purpose is always to love. This is why we are here. Remember, we are not human beings having a spiritual experience, we are spiritual beings having a human experience.

Teach your children love through experience, not language. The quagmire of vocabulary is limiting and imprisoning. In allowing experience as a teacher in this classroom of life, you are opening the door to infinite possibilities of growth. You and your children are in this world to expand beyond the vocabulary of self that you were taught. This is part of the re-wiring. You need to identify your natural self. You are not your mother. You are not your father. You are not your past life situation. If you are someone that has been exposed to violent acts of abuse growing up and see it today as normal or okay, then you will need to re-wire. This behavior is not okay. The fact that you experienced this in your upbringing, does not mean it is acceptable behavior. The goal for you will be to break the pattern. In doing so, you will learn to communicate with love, as you speak the truth in love. Using our hands to hit, is not an expression of love. Hands are to be used righteously, to comfort, to serve, and to heal. If you find yourself in a circumstance where the old pattern begins to emerge, it may require you to walk away in silence, until you are able to return to a conscious state of presence. The point is, a conscious shift must take place in order to break the mold for generational blessings.

All relationships are teachers. They are all experiences that are transient and provide opportunities for learning and growth. The constitution of marriage can be viewed as a double edged sword. It can bring Divine love into your daily experiences, or it can bring mortal fear into your daily experiences. There is an old saying that some marriages are made in heaven, and some are made in hell. Metaphorically speaking, this is true. Although most of us have the best intentions and imagine they will be married happily ever after, we are just not there yet as a collective society. Maybe one day. If we can learn to live life mindfully, in a state of presence, knowing that love is the heartbeat of life itself, then perhaps it can be a reality for many marriages to come. In my personal experience, the challenges I faced were necessary for evolution to take place in my life. If we had no tests or challenges in life, we would not evolve. It is that simple. The universal law of relativity states that we all receive these tests and challenges of initiation for the purpose of strengthening the light within. What I learned is that we must always remain connected to the heart as we move through an experience in order to find solutions to these life issues. Don't say or think "My life stinks." Instead, understand that these situations and occurrences are not your life. Life lives eternally at the heart center. It is not an external occurrence. There may be current situations in your life, but they are not your life. You are life. And you have the power within you to move through any life situation. There isn't a situation in the world that is more powerful than presence. Your presence can move mountains.

When there is a divorce, regardless of the horrific happenings during the marriage, children will still feel a degree of pain and separation, even if they have suffered a lot during the family's time together. Every child at one point in their young life dreams of their mom and dad together living happily ever after. Don't kid yourself by believing otherwise. It seems to be a natural desire. So be mindful of the children and protect their hearts, even in divorce. Remember they love you both. Even if a parent has been judged to do wrong by the child, the child deep down longs for love and acceptance from that parent at a much deeper level. Understand that the parent they experienced love with all along, has already shown their love and acceptance. Conversely, the child will chase and seek love and acceptance from the parent who they have lacked from, no matter how unworthy you have judged them to be. It is not for us to judge. Everyone is worthy of love. Remember, we want to remove the added stories that are attached to the pain so we can stop the suffering and come into peace. So don't hate on a child's mom or dad. Don't ask them to route for a team. The best thing a father can ever teach a young child, is the expression of love for their mother, even in divorce, and vice versa. You don't want their grown up hearts to be full of the things they heard as children. That only creates more pain that lives on inside of them for years and will affect them as adults. Be silent and allow the child's heart to intuitively guide them back to the only thing that matters, which is love. It costs nothing to show love. It costs everything not to.

Do Not Let Your Dreams Fade

I was fifteen years of age and it was just me and my mom left at home for the most part. They were tough years. Our roles somewhat reversed, as I found myself raising an adult child that was very much in pain, depressed, and curious about the world around her. She began hiding her pain behind an over-consumption of alcohol. This was a road I had never been down and was just learning how to drive myself. The ride was bumpy, and the sky was murky at times. Life was questionable for me. I was dubious in my role as an adult child, but I complied. I saw no other way around it, so instead, I went through it. Sometimes that's the only option. I kept my pace as the drizzle fell on my head. I imagined that eventually, the sun would have to shine through. After all, it can't all be bad. I am pretty certain this chapter of my life, however, added more suffering as I convinced myself that I was still being ripped off, and deserved a better teen age experience. Those thoughts did not help me manifest anything except more emptiness, and disillusion about family and parenting. The good news was that my personal dreams and visions were still clear. In fact, holding onto them is exactly how I manifested them. Having said that, it proved to me how powerful the mind truly is, no matter what circumstances are surrounding you.

We had financial difficulties and were considered poor. I was well aware that there were many other families that were worse off. This awareness lessened the 'woe is me' attitude that was knocking on the door of my brain. However, we did struggle. I remember going to the electric and lighting company across the street from my house and sat on the only empty chair available along with ten or so other adults all waiting to be seen by a representative in regards to their utility bills. I was the only child waiting. I was fifteen and was there to represent my mother and me. My mission was to get on a payment plan so we were not overwhelmed, did not get our service shut off, and not fall further behind in what we owed. These were the adult issues that I tended to as a teenager growing up. I took on my first job a few months before my sixteenth birthday, while I was still in high school. The fast food establishment was in view's eye from my home, where I started slinging hamburgers, dropping fries in oil, and running the cash register. My best friend at the time was also employed there, so good memories were made and it panned out as a fun experience. A few months later, I went on to a union job as a cashier in a large supermarket for some years after that while I finished High school. My school grades dropped in the last two years of high school. My mind was crowded and cluttered with confusion, and I did not have any guidance or mentor in my life at the time. I was unaware of the options I might have for onward education, as a financially underprivileged teen. My mother was busy working a full-time job and was out early on weekday mornings. Many times I slept through the alarm clock that went on for sixty minutes those mornings, and rarely made it to school on time. I imagine that all of the transitions I experienced at the time robbed my energy and hid my ability to feel motivated and focused on school work. My mental vision was obscured and I just couldn't see that far ahead of the environment around me. I was free from the past abuse and tension and was grateful for that. However, once the waves washed the violence from our home away, a new set of waves rolled in. There were many variables that were added to the mix. There were the dealings of my mother and her depression, the nonchalance of loved ones, and the arising of a relationship which emerged into my first love experience. These situations were compiled with finishing high school, working out of necessity, and trying to find my own way. My natural drive was for dance, and so that is what I focused on. I went to school because I had to graduate, went to work because I had to earn money, and continued studying in dance classes because it was my passion. Not only did dance class become my sanctuary, but it was my foundation. I knew that I needed to become fluent if I were going to reach my goal as a professional performer. The competition in New York City was fierce and I felt that my approach needed to involve two things. Do the best that I could, and do it the best that it could be done. This strong sense of focus and passion changed my current situation because I was focusing on my dreams. When I graduated, I continued to work, and a few years later my first love broke my heart with infidelity. It hit me like a ton of bricks. All that I loved and depended on was my love of dance and my love for him. So this break-up was to be the game changer that I didn't have on my to-do list for life. At that point, my dance career became the focal point. I went full speed ahead. I was teaching dance classes at night, and pounding the pavements by day in Manhattan. I remember making cheese sandwiches in my kitchen and putting it into my dance bag with some bottled water as I got ready for my journey into Manhattan. I would take it out and eat it on the train on my way in before classes and auditions. Money was still very tight, but my mom always had a chunk of processed American cheese in the fridge along with my favorite grain bread. It was the only meal that I could throw together for food on the go, and it filled me up. I grew to love cheese at the time, so it was really doable for me. That became my typical caloric intake before classes. I was on a role with auditions and sensed a streak of success coming my way. It was around that time when my cousin mentored me and helped me apply and get accepted into a College in Brooklyn, New York. It was the same cousin who called the family meeting with all of us children and our mom, several years before. The conditions were that I had to work in the college for a certain amount of hours a day, after classes, and use the time after that for studies. I didn't see where there would be time to audition in Manhattan. This left me in the cross roads of my mind. I needed to make a choice. After discussing it with my one of my brothers who was also a dancer, I decided to go with my heart, my intuition, and his advice which was to stay on the audition track that I was already on. In doing so, I manifested my dream to be a performer in NYC and Hollywood. I never let my dreams fade. It took some years, but the drizzle did stop and the sun did burst through. Buddha says there are three things that can't hide for long. The moon, the sun, and the truth. I was beginning to see that.

Performing Days

It was a chilly autumn morning. The sun had risen. Thousands of auditionees lined up like cattle as they hugged around the brick and mortar of the Minskoff rehearsal studios on Broadway in the billboard ridden theater district of Manhattan, New York. I was not new to the auditioning process and was aware that this was a cattle call and an amazing opportunity to graze new pastures. This particular casting call brought positive hype and excitement due to the Hollywood notoriety and glitz that it promised. All of the young hopefuls came out of the wood work. There were also dancers there that I knew from classes and other auditions. Typically in New York City, you saw many of the same people at the same auditions, all trying out for the same roles as you. But it was every man for himself, so to speak, and I was comfortable in my skin as a competitor and eager to win. Looking back, this may have been the one area in life that I had no fear. I truly loved to dance, so there was no space for the illusion of fear. Winning this role was perhaps one of my biggest accomplishments. I didn't get there by accident. It started with a dream. Then years of dedication and hard work studying and perfecting my craft, maintaining a perfect dancer's body, and performing from my heart is what made it a reality. It was truly an exciting time for me. We were dance contestants on FOX TV's Star Search which was hosted by the late celebrity, personality, and host Ed McMahon in Hollywood, California. The lights and cameras, and behind the scenes energy of the show was tremendous. I fed off that energy like nothing I had ever experienced before. We lost the competition by a quarter of a point. There was a gathering afterward at the Hotel that the other performers were having in celebration of their wins that evening. They all asked me to go and I was honored to be there. My dance partners did not want to join. I quickly put on my trendy white jumpsuit and raced off to find Ed McMahon back in the studio. Still, on fire from the ball of energy that was spinning inside of me, I found him at front stage right, standing just outside the wings in his black tuxedo. I approached him with my big candy red smile and asked him if he would take a picture with me, even though I was one of the losers. He put his arm around my right shoulder and said, "There are no losers that make it here, Lily. Only winners." I never forgot those words, and I knew he was being sincere. The photograph that we took together that night, continues to reside framed on my desk today, even after all of these years. No matter how many times I have moved in the past years, that photograph came with me. It inspired me and reminded me that I was a winner, even in the losses.

Back in New York and pumped up for my next auditions, I was ready for my next opportunity. A week or so later I won another dance audition which brought me on an interesting journey that I will never forget. I was hired as a showgirl dancer with Ringling Brother's Barnum & Bailey Circus. It was a one-year dance performer's contract. I was told to pack four seasons of clothing in one bag and of course dance attire and character shoes to rehearse in. Once contracts were delivered and signed, a one-way ticket to Florida was sent immediately after. So, I said my farewells and got packing. I was ready to live on the road and meet other girls just like myself. This was the first time I left my mom on her own, and although she had made some great positive changes in her life, it concerned me. But I knew this was my opportunity to experience the life that I dreamed of and was perhaps her opportunity to find herself too.

The New Year had just arrived. It was January 1985 in the dead of winter, and a cold one at that. By the time I bid farewells to all of my friends and was packed and ready for my adventure, I became very ill. My mother was worried and frowned against my continued plans in getting to the airport and onto a flight with a near fever. Regardless of the concern, I went. After all, it was my next new journey and a job I was expected to arrive for. When the wheels hit the runway, I followed the other passengers out of the aircraft and into the bright, crowded terminal. My eye sight became blurry as the brightness faded, and I began to feel faint. "Just breathe and focus" I kept telling myself. Through the crowd of travelers, I saw a hand holding a medium size white sign with my name on it. Focusing my eyes in closer, I saw the hand attached to a man wearing a Ringling Brother's Barnum & Bailey jacket. I approached the gentleman, stopped, put my bag down and forced a simulated smile on my pale white face. He asked, "Are you, Lily Sanders?" I replied, "Yes sir. And I need to get to a hospital..." and fainted. The man swooped me up and took me straight to the hospital. I don't recall which I was feeling most, but for certain, I was feeling both embarrassed and grateful. I remember the gentleman taking care of everything from the insurance forms to getting the medication I needed. He couldn't have been more efficient, as I was totally useless in caring for myself at the time. I was seen by a doctor, given antibiotics, and told I had pneumonia. He handed me a doctor's note, which was required as per my contract with the Production Company for Ringling Brothers Barnum & Bailey Circus. It stated my diagnosis, what medicine I was prescribed, and the required bed rest that I needed before going back to work. This meant I was unable to begin rehearsals and would be missing most of it before taking the show on the road. I was driven to their winter quarters where the train cars were kept. He drove up to train car #84, took my luggage from the trunk and popped it up onto the vestibule of the train car. The cars were not on any platform, so it was a large step up to get onto the car itself from ground level. The gentleman went up first, and I followed, pulling my weak body up with force as I held onto the side rail with all of my might. We walked into the train car from the left entrance. Down the corridor of the quiet train were closed pocket doors to my right and to my left. Each door was numbered. At the opposite end of the car was a kitchen. To the right, there was a sink, a convection oven, and a microwave. To the left was a wall of tiny refrigerators. There were about ten in all. Two showgirls were assigned to one refrigerator. Two numbers representing two showgirls were tagged on each miniature fridge for sharing. In the middle of the train car were two sliding pocket doors next to each other on the same side of the car. Each with just a toilet in it. There was an unpleasant smell in there. After the quick twenty five cent tour, he walked back to the room that he dropped my bag in front of previously and rambled, "Okay, Lily. Here you are. That is the fridge you will share which has your number on it, and the kitchen is communal. First come first serve. The girls seem to work it out. You can get food in the dining car once the show is on the road if you don't feel like cooking. There are no guys permitted in the Showgirls car. These are the toilets. Over here is your room. Room number thirteen. You are showgirl thirteen, so everything that relates to you will be numbered as such. Your room, fridge, your costumes, your shoes. Everything." He slid open the pocket door to my room. It was six feet by three feet with a large window. It seemed large anyway because the room was so small. It was basically like a closet with a sink and a window. He continued, "You have this window which you will want to dress and cover for privacy. Here is your sink and mirror to the right, and this is your bed." The bed was a thin mattress on top of a wooden bench-like compartment. He lifted up the wooden bench cover that was beneath the mattress and said, "This is your storage. It's not much, but feel free to put up whatever you need on the walls to store other things and make it home. Our shuttle bus picks up here every morning and goes to the building where the show is being rehearsed, and the production offices are. You'll meet your stage manager, production manager, general manager, and your choreographer there. Your producer will be there too. I will deliver the doctor's note to your manager. Here is your rehearsal schedule. There will be an earlier bus if you choose to get something to eat at the cafeteria before rehearsal, or the later bus which will get you there just before rehearsal begins. Don't miss that bus. It is your only way to rehearsal. Any questions?" I thought a moment and asked, "Yes. Where do I shower?" "At the building…" he says as he starts to walk away toward the same entrance we entered. "And where is everyone now?" I asked loudly. "At the building creating the greatest show on earth..." he replied, and off he went.

I lied on my back, staring up with my dizzy head at the train room ceiling. I felt like I had just joined the army. All I could wonder is why I wasn't told to bring sheets, towels, toiletries, eating utensils, plates or anything of this nature. I didn't even have a cup to take my antibiotics with. How was I even going to eat, I wondered? So I didn't. I fell asleep in that position till suddenly the sounds of eighteen dancing ladies giggling their way down the corridor woke me. The swooshing sounds of their room doors opening and closing, and girls piled high in laughter in someone's six by three closet peaked my attention. I could hear them laughing about their day and the muffled sounds of pouring cold drinks and cooking in the kitchen at the far end of the car. There were friendships bonding outside my room and the only thing bonding with me was the medicine and bile on the floor of my empty stomach. It was time for my evening dose, so I cupped my left hand beneath the sink, turned on the faucet with my right hand and down the hatch it went. This was a nightmare, I thought. Five days went by and I got weaker and weaker because I was losing weight fast. I was already thin before I left with a perfect show girl body. Now I imagine I was looking emaciated. Literally, I was starving. At this point, I had still not met anyone. I missed the entire week of choreography and missed the fittings for my costumes and head pieces. I missed everything. So what was I to do? One day while the girls were at the building rehearsing, I became nauseous from all of the medication in my empty stomach. I took slow steps to the toilet in the middle of the train car to vomit. Nothing but bile from the pit of my stomach came out. I had to eat something, so I continued to the kitchen to find the fridge with number thirteen on it. As I opened it up, I saw it filled with a large bottle of natural apple juice, a bunch of grapes, some bread, and other things that I don't recall. I took a piece of bread and went back to my room to wash it down with water from my sink. Now I have no choice but to open my door tonight and reach out to my refrigerator partner to tell her I was the mouse in her fridge. It was time anyway. I needed to ask for help so I can get food, towels, and also get to a phone booth. That night the showgirls came galloping in as usual, and at the usual time. I heard some girls outside of my room whispering. "That's the sick girl from New York." I felt embarrassed. I was also feeling shy and alone, but mostly starving. When everyone settled in and things became quieter, I slid my door open and stood up. A beautiful girl that was in the room next to mine on the right, saw me immediately and greeted me warmly. "Hi! How are you? We have all been worried about you." I replied, "Hey. I'm hanging in. Thank you. Is it possible for me to borrow a cup, please? I need to take my pills and drink some water. I have been using my hands and nothing to eat." She was very kind. She made me a cup of delicious hot tea and served it to me in a colorful large ceramic coffee mug. She told me to use that mug until I get my own things. Then a taller girl comes skipping down to my room. Alas, I met my refrigerator partner. She was a big girl, full of confidence and spunky in character. I told her that I helped myself to bread in the fridge and would be happy to replace it as soon as I could get to a supermarket. I explained that I needed to get some things like food and other necessities, and asked her where everyone was shopping. A few other girls heard us and walked to my room to meet and greet me. I remember giving money to one girl that was sympathetic to my needs, and off she went with my list of things. I tried to think of things that didn't need refrigerating like fresh fruit, dry cereal, and small bottles of iced tea. By hook or by crook, however, I was squeezing in a container of milk because I was dying for a cup of coffee. And that I did. It was now the weekend and I was able to get the bus to the building and shower. I began to feel somewhat human again. But I also remember feeling like giving up for the first time. I missed all of the choreography for the week, and the next week was a matter of rehearsing everything they were just taught. How was I to catch up? I assumed that most of the girls had begun friendships and were bonding with each other, and wondered how I would ever blend in. Fear set in. I believed everything that fear was telling me, and asked one of the showgirls to ask our manager to come to the train car that Monday to talk with me about my current position. I was planning to break my contract and go back to New York. The girls went off to rehearsal and I stayed resting in my room. The good news is, that I was beginning to feel better and stronger. I hear a voice of a woman calling out my name as she walks down the train corridor toward my room. I open the pocket door and there stood a tall full bodied woman with bright blue smiling eyes behind spectacles. I scooted over a few feet and patted my hand on the thin mattress gesturing her to sit beside me. She did. She introduced herself to me. She was the kindest woman, in full acknowledgment and acceptance of how ill I was and how much I had already missed. She was also business minded and firm. The conversation went something like this: "So Lily, what's on your mind?" she asked. I said, "Well, I was thinking that I only have five days left to learn this choreography and get fitted for costumes and head pieces. I was wondering if I would be allowed out of my contract and perhaps be replaced." She said something like this, "Well, you can quit and go home. I certainly can't stop you. You could leave, go back to New York never knowing if you could have done it. Or you can stay, knowing that you have the professional ability to learn everything. Your choreographer you auditioned for, said you are quite capable of learning quickly and doing a great job at that. So, you have a choice. Give up and get on a first flight home, or get on the early bus in the morning and start finding your place in the show." I was speechless and took a moment. I remember going inside my head and having a total conversation with my ego. I am not a quitter. How could she say that? Another beat went by. She's right. This would be giving up. Why would I ever do that? Of course, I am capable of learning it. I could do it easily. I'll prove it. With that, I replied with a smile, "Okay. I'll stay. And I won't let you down." "Great! See you in the morning?" she asked. "Yes. See you in the morning." I replied. Before she left, she instructed me to eat something in the cafeteria, go down to the controller to sign something for my paychecks, and get to wardrobe so I can be measured. She said I was to do this all before meeting up with the other showgirls in rehearsal. I assured her that I would. As she walked away, I called out to her with sincere gratitude. "Thank you." She turned to me and humbly smiled as she left the train car. This woman wound up being one of the kindest, smartest, and most professional people I had encountered that year. It was no accident that my journey started with such challenges. It was a valuable lesson about the choice between fear and love that I needed to learn. It may appear to be a choice between quitting and persevering, but truly it was about fear and love. She spoke truth into me that day in car #84. If it weren't for her, I may have missed the amazing opportunity that was before me. I chose to trust myself and my ability to do what I love, and let go of the fear that was telling me it's too late and I am too weak. Love triumphed over fear on this day.

That evening I announced to the other showgirls that I was not leaving for New York after all and would be starting rehearsal the next day. They were excited to see me stay and it was comforting to feel the love and support. One of the girls, who was to become one of my best friends, was inspiring. She was a lovely gal from Maryland and had more spirit than anyone. She sat on her bed, with a smile from ear to ear as I stood outside her room looking over her. She told me that as soon as I show up to the building and hear the live band, see the all of the lights, and watch all the choreography coming together…I was going to remember why I came. She was completely right. I was trapped in that six by three room by myself for seven days without any food or human contact. I latched on to fear and was looking to escape. I was also starving. All I needed to do was accept the situation and do something to change it for the better. The choice I made was to abandon fear and return to what I loved. Dance. This was my dream, after all. It was a very important lesson that I learned and am forever grateful to my manager for handling it the way she did. I imagine she sensed that I had lost myself in that little room while I lied there sick for days. Instead of pampering me, she decided to use the very words that changed my mind. The concept of quitting or giving up was not something I was about to adopt. So I went on to experience my journey as a showgirl, and it has taught me much about love and fear. When we hold onto our dreams and never let them go, they really can happen. But we cannot just dream about it in our minds, we must hold onto the love and passion we have for something and use it as a catapult that takes us to the very steps needed for manifestation in our lives. All of the what if's that fear was telling me, were decoys from the truth. Not giving into the lies that my ego mind was telling me was the best antidote for moving on, because it allowed me to be true to myself. We must always be true to our natural self. Always. In that natural self, we can inspire and be inspired. We can imagine and create. We can laugh and make others laugh. We can cry and comfort others. Truly, the ring master's statement at the end of each show, *"May all your days be circus days"* took on a whole new meaning.

"In allowing experience as a teacher in this classroom of life, you are opening the door to infinite possibilities of growth."

~Lily Sanders

CHAPTER 4

The Path Left of Center

TEN YEARS HAD PASSED. The relationship with the British man was stagnant. Although we had a genuine friendship and had mutual loving respect for each other, we seemed to be on the same tracks moving in different directions. I moved on to live by myself and follow a path that headed back toward my dreams. I signed a rental lease for an awesome high rise apartment with a twenty-four-hour doorman, and a terrace that over looked the Manhattan Yacht Club and Marina. To the left, as I faced west, stood the iconic Statue of Liberty. This was downtown New York City, outside of the World Trade Center. That was where I wanted to be and so that was where I manifested a place to live. I knew that I needed to be living in the city to avail myself of the entertainment opportunities I sought after at the time. My heart jumped with joy over this new life I had begun. My mom called me daily, and I also spoke to my father often. I kept a part time day job with a group of talented and also peculiar actors and young hopefuls while auditioning and performing different gigs on television and film in Manhattan.

Leading into this time, I studied acting and different acting methods intensely. It was my one thing in life that I wanted and so this is what I did at all times outside of work and sleep until I eventually began to hit closer to my target, which was my passion. Deep down, I felt that this was my 'what'. I spent most of my time after and before work, learning different techniques and acting methods from the best coaches in New York City. The methods I learned included the popular Stanislavski, Strasberg, and Adler methods. Personally, I was still not satisfied with any of these techniques for a few reasons. One major reason was that I felt it leads the actor to become unconscious, as a performer. I don't believe emotional recall works every time, and I knew it was impossible to rely on. You cannot recapture what wowed last night's audience. It is just not possible. Additionally, how can I be present with another actor on stage when I am recalling the day my friend suffocated to his death in a house fire? Emotional preparation is important but it needs to come from a foundation and be built upon as the script is studied, and there is a deeper, organic space where one has the ability to connect with meaning. When this happens, the actor is prepared to take action no matter what happens in that moment on that particular night because the emotional domino has been set in place. The only thing you are doing is whatever activity you are directed to do, being acutely aware of what is really going on in the scene, and be responsive to the scene partners that are on stage with you. This is life on stage. I wanted a method that I could rely on that kept me organic. Authentic. Real. I wanted to express the moment at hand naturally where the only thing that is called upon is my heart in that moment. Just as this moment is all there ever is in life, it is also the key to life on the stage. I fervently searched and found it. It was to be Sanford Meisner's method, which kept me in the present moment. Ironically, this became a powerful tool for me for life itself. Being present. Being in the moment. The act of doing, and not perceiving. Acting is not talking about something or feeling something. Acting is doing. Acting is being. This was to be the arising of a critical conscious shift in my life, although I did not know it at the time. When I became skilled and ready to go, I auditioned for opportunities which landed me key roles. I landed a wonderful opportunity with a theatrical company downtown and journeyed with them playing leading roles in three Off Broadway dramatic and comedic productions. Later, I became a regular day player on a daytime ABC soap opera. I knew I was on my way to bigger and better things.

What I didn't know was that it was an opportunity for a very important healing time for me, and was also an opportunity for self-discovery. Lastly, it was a free invitation into the classroom of life, learning to love myself, and honor myself for who I was and where I have gotten to after all that I had experienced prior. There were deep seated emotional wounds from my upbringing, and also from the loss and separation of my first love that I was unaware of at the time. There was an emptiness that needed my full inward attention. I had begun somewhat of a spiritual journey in my searching, but all that I read and heard was still not clicking. I wasn't ready to evolve. There were thoughts in my mind that I was not aware of. These were the thoughts of my ego. I couldn't see them, but somehow they were visible inside of me and took residence there in my mental warehouse. Many were painful thoughts that rested there on shelves. And every time my mind went to a painful memory, this little man I will call the warehouse manager would grab a thought and fling it over to me. Hard! So as life situations would have it, I was thrown a curve ball and had no idea how to catch or dodge it. Instead, I exercised my free will and for the most part, moved into an unconscious relationship ignoring who I was and what my purpose was. This was an astounding time of my life.

Within a short time, I fell in love and found myself in a highly controlling marriage with a man I had only just begun to know and understand. It was full speed ahead, and I got caught up in this wind tunnel that blinded me from myself. There was a blankness, and suddenly I lost all grips of who I was and any sense of individuality or oneness with the Universe. It was my first experience in a co-dependent relationship. In truth, at this point in my life journey, I had not yet learned to love and trust my inner child. Instead, I depended on someone else to love me, in order for me to love myself. Perhaps this is a familiar feeling for you, as the reader. This contributes to losing your identity. There becomes an absence of a connection between you and your inner child. Being in a marriage of co-dependency will divorce you from your Self. This is a deadly trade off.

I began to identify myself as the paint brush that absorbed all the colors of the pallet magnificently, so the artist could create something beautiful with me onto his canvas. I did not feel life included me anymore. I became the magic wand for weaving colors across his canvas. An artist's paint brush becomes a beloved tool the more they use it. As they paint they will become increasingly familiar with the way the brush handles the paint and what it can accomplish for them. Pretty soon that paint brush will become a part of them that they will intuitively know how to successfully maneuver it as they wish. I trust that this analogy makes sense to you, as this is my abbreviated version of how and why people experience a controlling relationship. It also explains co-dependency. How can an artist paint on his canvas without his magic wand? Without his beloved tool? And how can the beloved tool be useful unless it's in the hands of an artist? This is because many of us have been programmed to look for, rely on, and expect that another human being is supposed to paint our happy story.

Societal and cultural conditioning of the mind goes beyond marital relationships. Many expect the love of an infant baby to bring happiness to oneself, or to an unfulfilled partnership. Then the moment the baby is born and becomes colic, or for any number of reasons the infant is crying all the time or has physical or mental challenges, the couple spins further into a web filled with stress, weariness, frustration and fighting as they continue to add to their unhappiness.

Many people seek out happiness in a continuous search cycle they call life, where nothing on the ground in which they are standing is honored, and everywhere they have not stood is sought after because the mind tells you that this is where happiness lies. But in reality, it is all an illusion. The only thing that is real, is where you are at this moment. Outwardly things appear normal, or at least as good as it's going to get. Meanwhile there is the voice of thought in the head that refuses to say it will be happy until you get that girl or guy, you've paid off your student loans, you get your doctorate degree, you own your production company, you get the yacht, you become a grandparent, you retire and move to Italy...and so on. You go through the motions appearing happy, but there is this background static of perpetual discontent. You become so used to the static that you no longer hear it. It all seems so normal. Why is that? Because you are always looking to get there when you are here. You are always wanting that when you have this. And the whole time, while you are striving and reaching and wanting and seeking, and waiting for that day to come, you are missing the point. You are missing the purpose. You bypass the moment. You don't see what is in the now because it is clouded over by the mind's perception of reality. When you can fully go beyond the thinking mind, and accept what is, you can become grateful for the reality of the present moment. Grateful for the breath of life, for who you are, and for what simply is. To have gratitude for what is, and the many blessings in life is truly a virtue.

Being financially dissatisfied may motivate you to get rich, but even if you do make millions you will continue to feel a lacking, and inner non-fulfillment. You will probably have awesome things and experience exciting places, but those things come and go. In between it all you will always feel empty. That is because you have conditioned your mind to seek fulfillment and happiness in the future, which doesn't

even exist. The future only exists in the mind. The unfulfilled 'self' lives only in the mind's relationship with it. It is
buying into a script that it is constantly pitching you. If you
believe this script as the play of your life, then you will feel
stuck in it, while you wait for something better and bigger to
come along. And yet, it never really comes. It never comes
because happiness is found in the moment of living, not in the
moment of waiting. Give up waiting as a state of mind. Although it is good to know the path you are traveling, you must
always be mindful of the step you are taking at this moment.
The journey is each step, one step at a time, to be observed,
accepted, and appreciated. All of the bumps in the road and
even the darkest of caves can be used as a significant tool to
the arising of your natural essence. In philosophy, it is said
that 'essence is the attribute or set of attributes that make an
entity what it fundamentally is, and which it has by necessity,
and which without it loses its identity'. That natural essence
is timeless and without form. Everything else in the external
world is of form and relates to the hands on the clock. These
things have their place within the world of form and are to be
appreciated and respected, but they can never give you lasting
fulfillment because it is always changing as time goes by.

Even if you don't want it to, it must. It is always subject to
time. Things come and go, and so do the people in our lives.
That said, it is safe to suggest that because we can
acknowledge the differences between form and formless
things in life, we can also see the differences in our purposes
too. In this respect, we can really see how we have two purposes in life. Our first purpose is our soul's purpose, which is
to be fully here and aligned with the truth of this moment.
Your soul purpose is the momentous purpose. It is vital in its
immediate direction that lines you up for the next moment,
and the one after that, and so on. It is kind of like the internal
domino that falls onto the next domino in Divine placement
as it continues into infinity. With a soul purpose, there are no
means to an end. It wears no watch and takes no form. It just
keeps on going into the hands of infinity. I like to see it as the
shapeless space that encompasses each moment. Even each
moment will come and go, but that is the beauty of it. You
are not trapped in it. Each breath is enlightenment. A new
awakening. You are able to realize your soul purpose in life
without arranging it, and without it being subject to clock
time. Once you come to this realization, you can give up the
expectation of things that you believe should make you happy

and fulfilled. Instead, you can begin to make those purposes in the world of form secondary to your soul purpose. In my view, your external purpose should always be guided by your soul purpose. There is no greater satisfaction than when you have a career that is guided by your heart. This is life mastery. We are all capable of this. We need to make the conscious choice to awaken and evolve into this ever present life, as we step from moment to moment, and experience to experience. When we shift our mindset and go deeper, we can do this.

People are creatures of habit. Most of us wake up at the same time. You hurry up and get ready to get on the same train or bus, or get into your vehicles at the same time and take the same route to work. You race off to stand in line at the same coffee joint, and then scurry back to the car only to sit in the same usual traffic while tuning into the same morning news. You hurry to pick up the kids at this game or that event and cook the usual tacos on Tuesdays. You sit in the same chair and watch the same Television programs and then go to sleep on the same side of the bed. Then you wake up and do the same thing all over again. Is it any wonder why we don't evolve? How can we want change in our lives when we are doing the same thing every day? If we program our mind and body to do the same thing every day, the heart will tag along. And then one day you wake up and ask yourself, "Who am I? What is this all about?" Suddenly you realize that your life is no different than the character Phil Conner, where every day is "Ground Hog Day". This 1993 film is a wonderful expression of how the same system, the same thoughts, the same behavior and the same choices today, become your tomorrow. So it is safe to suggest that the same mindset we hold onto from the past creates our future. We have to change the system if we want to see a different result. What is the internal dialogue in your brain? When is the last time you visited your heart? And what intuitive actions will you take in order to have positive change and transformation in your life? These were my personal questions that fueled my search for love, happiness, and fulfillment.

What I learned was that the soul's purpose must always be first in line, and the external purpose follows. The soul's purpose is the first domino that sets the others in motion. As this happens, there is a beautiful symphony in the connection between the heart, intuition, and the brain. Even writing this book, has been very much in the spirit of the moment, and has not come from thought as much as it just flows from the spirit and has innately landed these pages.

So how does this apply to relationships, partnerships, and marriages? Everywhere, every day, and every moment. Your relationships are not your purpose, rather a portal that gives you the opportunity to express the Divine given gift of love to oneself, and toward others. You must first love yourself, with sincere enthusiasm in order to stand on your own and express true love to another. All relationships are experiences, and these experiences are our teachers. When you can recognize thwarting, wanting, and needing in a relationship, then you will recognize the ego. Today there is a large amount of negative discussion and teachings on the concept of the ego. It is not that the ego is right or wrong, or good or bad. It's that the ego can operate unconsciously because it contains both unconscious, preconscious and conscious elements. In respect to the ego driving a relationship, it is not the essence of that person who is loving you but perhaps the unconscious ego of that person controlling you. When you are living with someone who has emotional pain from past experiences that are highly active, they tend to be either aloof or volatile all the time. This is an important lesson that I learned through experience. Conversely, control can be easily masked in silence as a seemingly harmless co-dependent relationship. It is not the essence of you falling for that person, but the unconscious hidden pain in you relating to the pain in another. It is almost like the common denominators in two people finding each other and hanging out because it somehow feels familiar. They begin to actually feed off each other. We all carry some level of hidden emotional pain. If someone is not violent, it doesn't mean that they do not have emotional pain. The pain can often be dormant, waiting for someone's seductive ego to come along and engage. Ego takes on the form of many costumes. This is why it is critical to grasp this understanding so that you can remain present when the enemy attacks, so to speak. Recognizing the ego's presence can be used as an opening to transcend a co-dependent, controlling, or violent relationship whether you are a child, an adult, a spouse or a partner. This will require you to become completely tuned in. In that state of awareness, you will become a witness of a situation instead of a victim of it. When you are tuned in and completely present, you will know that these actions you observe are not the source of love, but the diminishing of it.

We are not here to treat or be treated by others in an unloving way. We are not here to cause suffering, and we are not here to fall victim of someone's pain. We are only here to express love.

That said, experiencing a relationship can be simple. A relationship can beautifully blossom quickly or can grow slowly at its own unique pace. It is not the amount of time that you give a relationship that is needed to know if it's real or not. Remember, reality is in the now. I believe we can all find love in a moment. It is the qualia of each moment, in each experience together that can be natural and alert in expression. When you can be fully conscious of an experience with another beyond the surface of the mind, the potential is there to grow it into a deeper or heightened relationship together. When you are very conscious, where you are no longer subject to a mental picture or representation of another, there can be qualia. You can experience the intrinsic features in another and find beauty in everything, regardless of how much or little time you spend together. This took me decades to learn. Well worth the wait, as I can say today that the concept of being in a relationship is no longer tentative for me. I embrace love and welcome being in a loving relationship where I have no fears for tomorrow, no regrets from yesterday, and only joy in the moment. Before I came to this place, however, there seemed to be more experiences that I needed to have.

Baby

My body was ready to enter into a whole new dimension. Eager to experience and stride through this journey, I wrapped my heart around the very concept of diaper changing and nursing, and the honor that comes with loving and nurturing a little bundle from heaven. Although I was not a single minded being at the time, the one thing I was aiming toward and determined to accomplish was motherhood. I had a good sense of intuition that consciously anchored in the forefront of my mind's eye. I knew this was to be at some point in life, and although I had just miscarried it was only a matter time before coddling a new born would manifest. I remember I was working on the set of ABC's One Life to Live, and I had received the call from my obstetrician that I was pregnant again, and that this time the chromosome count looked more promising. As I darted off to the public phone which was just off set, there was a slight discomfort in my emotions as I began to call my husband. Although sharing the good news was what I wanted, I remember feeling a sense of reluctance as the dense morning air had been lingering inside of me. Signs of disapproval filled the cottage that morning, as I raced to catch a train into New York City to work. One could cut the tension in the air with a knife. I picked up the phone handle and put in coins. Feeling my heart rate rise and a pounding in my chest, I remember wondering if it was the hormones kicking in or fear. It was a disturbing feeling. I always imagined that telling your husband you are pregnant was to be a celebratory announcement. Why couldn't I feel that I wondered? Could it be that I married someone that carried similar patterns as my father? I bit the bullet, pushed the numbers on the keyboard of the public phone near the green room and waited as it rang. I told him the good news. I don't recall the entire conversation but I do recall an unenthusiastic response that went something like this: "Maybe you won't lose this one." This moment seemed to set the stage for our short union.

I gave birth to a healthy and beautiful baby boy, who we both loved and adored endlessly. I nurtured him around the clock, and my love for him measured from here to the moon, around the Universe and back again. My role as a full-time nursing mother was welcomed, and although it was a full-time job, it never felt like work. It was an enormous gift I was given that opened my heart to a new and exciting place where observing and engaging in the baby's love and growth filled the pumping chambers of my heart.

Mother's Day

It was my 2nd Mother's Day, and my husband suggested we drive down to the south shore that morning with the baby to see his mother. When we arrived and knocked on the door, there was no answer. Distorted facial expressions leaped from my husband's face as I stood on the stoop with the baby in my arms. Down the cracked cement stoop and across the lawn he went, as he headed back toward the truck. The passenger door slammed shut. I followed behind in silence, secured our bundle of joy into the car seat, and planted myself in the empty seat behind the wheel. As I drove off, darts flew from the right, as blame and name calling began to minimize me. I remember feeling my insides shrink, and imagined myself as the incredible shrinking woman. The one-way conversation went something like this, "This is your fault that we came all the way down here for nothing, and now we have to keep the baby in the car all the way back home. Way to go Lil. You couldn't take the time or have the decency to call my mother and tell her we would be coming to see her on Mother's Day. You waste my time on my weekends that I have such little time to spend with my son and my mother because all you can think about is your selfish little self. You're pathetic." I continued to drive and shrink even more. It was an emotional route back home, enduring thirty minutes of badgering and shouting until tears streamed out and poured over me. The cries of a baby in distress bounced off the walls of the truck and echoed in my ears. Peace was robbed by the wail of anger's voice, leaving hearts confused and shattered. As I pulled up the long driveway of the wooded property in which we resided, he bolted out of the passenger seat, slammed the truck door behind him and fled to the cottage. I wiped the salted mascara from my cheeks and turned back toward the baby. He stared at me, with his loving blackish brown eyes that were waiting to be met with comfort. Dashing to the back seat for him, I went inward for whatever morsel of peace I could find. I always found it in there somewhere, so I could pour that sense of peace onto that teensy soul that I loved so dearly. This was no easy task, but I was pretty good at mastering comfort and solace for our child while suppressing the pain that danced around in the inner courtyard of my heart. My concern was for the needs of the baby and I am grateful that I was able to bounce back, for the most part. On this particular day, it was an artificial smile that showed up to comfort the baby, coupled with wholehearted loving as the warmth of my body embraced him skin to skin. What I found was that the physical act of smiling had quick recourse, as it transmuted into a peace that could only be described as presence. I hadn't yet awakened but I was experiencing glimpses of an awakening, as the presence of peace covered us. I was able to leave what just happened behind and let it go, for the sake of love and peace in that moment. There was great power in harmonizing the body with my heart and soul.

It was a beautiful crisp spring day and I recall the sun flooding the skies. My mind's desire was to change the mood in the cottage, but the air was so heavy, and it seemed that the Universe would not comply. I asked my husband if he wanted to take the baby to the park. He did not respond. I followed my heart and took an action that would change the air and energy that surrounded us. I put the baby in the car seat and drove to the harbor, which was a mile or so up the road. This took courage on my behalf. Most abusive people want their victims to be miserable in their presence because it feeds their pain even more. But the Universe had a different plan for me that day, and off we went. We strolled around the fishing pier and took in the smells of the salted waters and watched people frolicking around their boats tied to the high wooden docks. The sounds of the boats clanking on the sides of the slips as the water splashing back and forth was comforting. We observed the seagulls diving down and swooping up with whatever fish they could catch. They were full of energy and life, and nothing was stopping their next hunt and flight. I always took my son to the water. I am not sure why. To me, being surrounded by the earth's natural elements seemed closer to its Creator and brought me a sense of connectedness. Next stop was the park, just below the dock, where we playfully strolled to soon after. As we wheeled down the side walk, we took in the laughter of squirrels as they ran up and down the trees together. Upon our arrival to the playground, there were twenty or more smiling moms nearby their attentive husbands. There were crawling babies in the sand, climbing children on the teeter totters, adventurous toddlers going down the slides while giggling others went faster and faster on the merry go round. I sat on the wooden bench, with this little alert bundle of joy tucked in my lap. His chair on wheels stayed parked beside us, barring crumbs of Zwieback cookies and smashed apple pieces embedded in its blue cushions.

The western world suggests that mothers are to be honored on this particular day. Although the date was a traditional fixture on the calendar, I couldn't help but feel that my little world was not cooperating. As I sat on the bench watching all of the families, I remember imagining that I was in those scenarios. I admired the unity and the respect. I wished it were my husband waiting at the bottom of the slide clicking away on his camera. It wasn't the act of doing that I admired, as much as the act of love that I desired. I allowed the scene around us in the playground to make me feel relationship deprived. Conversely, I felt whole and complete as a mother. There was a sense of connection and cooperation that I had in motherhood. I needed nothing external to convince me of this. It was innate. I loved that child to the depth and width and height my soul could reach. And because of this, as long as I was internally connected with him and that true sense of being within myself, I could go on. I felt motherhood gave me purpose. This was the one relationship that was not deprived, rather I was blessed and privileged to behold this child and love him in all of its wonderment. This moment I knew was real and absolute. There was no struggle or conflict. It was pure and natural love. This was my understanding of infinite love.

As I recall, the environment at the playground saddened me. I wanted to cry to someone but felt I had no one. I was somewhat alienated from some of my family and friends as a result of my husband's ability to influence and control me. This was done by the use of isolation. If you or someone you know have ever been in a controlling or abusive relationship, then you understand exactly how that is done. What I do, who I hang out with, who I talk to, where I go, and limiting my involvement with the outside world that doesn't include him is what I allowed him to control. It was accomplished by mental coercion. An example would be him saying, "We move as one." That may sound loving and romantic to you readers, but try literately living that excuse for love and being forced to deny the natural flow of love as one individual loving another. To lose your inner voice, and the ability to express it outwardly stunts your spiritual growth. It's taking control of the marital foundation and hiding it behind a constitution called love. It's a lie. It's a sin. We all know that the word sin means to miss the mark. As I gazed into the beautiful blue sky with the baby in my lap, I couldn't help but be aware that this relationship was missing the mark. This was not my target. Conversely, it was the path left of center.

I felt I was a part of nothing, at this point. There was a sense of powerlessness that overcame me. All I was able to hear was a voice in my head telling me that this relationship was a failure, and I was too. I didn't know what to do about the situation, except try and fix it. As a child, I couldn't fix my parent's marriage and as a wife, I couldn't fix my own. What did all of this mean? Why was I giving up the power within me in a desperate attempt to gain love? It seemed to be learned behavior, and perhaps what was taught by my parents. It was the result of the conditioned mind patterns that were put in motion so many years ago, in a highly controlling, fearful and violent environment. However, having never addressed any of this from my years growing up, spun me into a tangled web of repeat. The control continued to multiply in my life, like a kaleidoscopic pattern that mirrored the experience before.

Moments of Presence, Moments to Cherish

Control became common behavior and at times I didn't know if I was coming or going. I recall my mom saying one day, "He has you on skates." Interesting observation and remark. Name calling became common as well, and I stored the degrading names in my mental warehouse. But by Divine favor, I always diverted my attention back toward moments of presence. Presence is important because infants and toddlers are well aware of negative energies and have the ability to sense everything. One of the worse things a person can do is upset a nursing mother. It has what I call a double negative effect because the stress goes directly from the mother and onto the baby. I nursed this tiny bundle of joy for exactly one year. One day, I remember my mother telling me not to nurse the baby when I am tense and upset. She was right. I am so grateful for her words of wisdom. I always remembered that and would take a moment to become present and connect to

Divine peace that I could only find within. Many times I was able to come into presence just by observing the baby's tiny fragile fingers, and his blackish brown eyes that always gazed at me in loving wonder. He absolutely took my breath away every time. Then I would nurse him.

One day while nursing, I had an esoteric experience that I have never discussed with anyone until now, as I type it on this keyboard. As he wrapped all five of his fingers around my one, I suddenly felt this lifted sensation. I knew we were not just connected as a family on earth but knew we were also connected as a family on a soul level. Perhaps this cannot be read with complete understanding, and can only be experienced. None the less, this was the experience I had. I knew at that moment that there was much more to life than this physical human experience on earth. That knowing brought me release from physical tension, but also there was a sense of openness that was once foreign to me. These moments of presence were moments to cherish. My fondest times were nursing the baby through the night by myself in the living-room, and being in complete peace looking down at his beautiful little everything that he possessed. My son didn't sleep through the night for two years. So it is safe to say that my days and nights with him filled my calendar. There was such little alone time, and the once simple things like shaving both legs during a shower became a challenge. By the time I finished half of one leg, that little walking bundle of joy was joining in as he climbed into the shower to meet his momma. These were comical and memorable experiences, and for the most part, it was definitely my happy place. I enjoyed every single sleepless second with him. I remember the very first day he slept through the night. When he woke, I looked into his blackish brown eyes and said softly, "Hi. I missed you last night while you were sleeping." These were joyful times as a mother, and also there were some nice moments as a wife. It can't all be bad. When things were good, they were good. Awareness of the good moments is a gift too. As infrequent as they may be, it is healthy and honest to recognize them.

The Soil that Rests on Solid Ground

If you want to bless your children, the energy of love must prevail. This was a powerful lesson that I learned through experience. If you think for one moment that your baby or toddler does not sense the turmoil, the coldness, the ignorance, the unkind acts, and the hate, then you are believing a lie that your mind has convinced you of. Hate may seem like a strong word to most readers, but there is no gray. If you are not expressing love, you are expressing hate. It's as simple as that. Love is not double sided. Love does not have good days and bad days. Love always prevails and takes the high road regardless of how low you are. Love is what the foundation of your marriage and your family home life should be built upon. The foundation should always be built on love. That's the good soil that rests on solid ground. If you build your house in the sand on the side of the hill, it will surely come down, no matter how much vegetation you've surrounded it with. If you build your house on solid, stable, good soil, it can withstand not only the weight and support on its foundation, but can also stay stable through wetting and drying cycles due to the environment, expanding and contracting without cracking the foundation. That foundation should also be able to withstand the precipitation life brings us, so that the run off and erosion which I call the minutiae in life, does not damage the structure of the marriage and family life you have built upon. When you have this balance of soil that you build your foundation on, no corrosion will set in. There are no damaging elements in love to gnaw away at. Love builds upon love. Hate cannot even withstand love. One of the single most important things to understand about love is that it is not a word. Love is an energy. And it is the most powerful energy in existence.

Hateful words and harmful actions are a recipe for division, not unity. Hate divides, while love unites. The lesson I learned here was to mind our words, and guard our thoughts, lest they come back to bite us. We may not be able to stop someone from being verbally unkind to us, however, if someone is always putting you down, don't put it in your memory bank. Instead, rebuke it. Because when negative and hateful words enter the mind, they become part of your thoughts. And when you are living with a thought based mentality, and you identify yourself with these thoughts, then the thoughts have the potential to control you. When you believe those illusory thoughts, it hides your truth. Diminishing words and name calling will stop hurting you when you rebuke them, and start loving yourself. To love yourself is to know yourself. But if you are identifying with names and thoughts you are given about yourself, who you really are will feel like a complete stranger to you. And how can you truly love someone you do not know? Can you see how critical it is to know and love yourself? It is really important to get honest with yourself. Because if you can be aware that you are identifying yourself with other people's words and labels, and even the ones you put on yourself, then you can begin to see how the ego's mind fights to control. Don't let it. Take charge of it and claim your truth. The constant inner battle between thought and reality, unconscious and conscious, will end as soon as you stop clinging to a thought-based identity. What other people say, and what your own thoughts tell you, is not your truth. Your truth is love. You are love.

CHAPTER 5

Hate and Revenge

HATE AND REVENGE CONTINUED during the divorce, and well after the divorce for years on end. The controversy smoldered on for several years. It was a nightmare for all involved. The constant harassment, being dragged in and out of the court all in the name of hate and revenge for a period of over fifteen years. How in the world can anyone raise a child with this insanity and what do you suppose a child will learn through these experiences? What I found is that no matter what the circumstances, had I just been in acceptance of all of the nonsense, I would have gotten to the same place without all of the suffering. Being in acceptance may not have gotten my baby back sooner when he was taken or lessened the number of court appearances, however, I would have had a sense of inner peace through it all. Acceptance brings a sense of peace that allows clarity of the mind and stillness of the heart. There is no greater resolve than peace. If there is anyone who can relate to the minutiae in divorce situations, learn from my lesson and just let it go. Be aware of the situation, and without judging it or others, let it go. The bottom line is that you maintain inner peace in all of it because your children need peaceful parents so they can feel peace as well. A lot of suffering can be eliminated if you can be in acceptance of what is, and then take the appropriate actions needed with grace and dignity. In the end, nothing righteous ever comes out from acts of hate and vengeance. Ever.

One day, my immediate family waited at my apartment on the Sunday of our son's fourth birthday to surprise him with a little cake celebration, and he was never returned home to me. This was to be one of many birthdays and holidays that we were unable to spend together as planned. The lesson I eventually learned was to detach from the highlights and labels the world puts on things. The holidays on the calendar soon became meaningless. We are taught that this day is special, and that holiday is to be revered. We put these days on paper and are told that we own it on this year and give it up on the alternate year. The court systems put it in writing, and it is suggested that as divorced parents, you are to abide by these dates as you raise the child and that this is your 'right'. It is stipulated. And then you are awarded these dates. Interesting choice of vocabulary this world teaches us. And we all buy into it. Literally. I am here to tell you otherwise. This is no reward. Rather, it is pure insanity. Imagine living life every day, subject to a piece of paper that the Supreme Court has stamped and sealed? Imagine that now you are teaching your child that his or her life is to be subject to this same paper? And imagine that you had to pay twenty thousand dollars or more to the attorney that managed your case and drew up these rules for all to abide by? Has the collective society gone mad? Actually, yes. This world has gone mad, and it is time for a collective awakening into a present state of consciousness, where there is an alert awareness that knows that none of these things of form really matter. I love birthdays. But truly, birthdays are every day. Every day we breathe, is the birth of a new day. Every moment we arrive at, births a new experience and a new opportunity to love and be loved.

In my view, this is the problem with being taught language rather than experience. We are taught that a structured world is a safe world. And yet, it is completely unstable. Did we not experience the horrific crumbling of the Twin Towers in New York City on September 11, 2001, as a result of a coordinated terrorist attack by al-Qaeda on the United States of America? One of the most recent tsunamis I remember was in March 2011. It happened off the Pacific coast of Japan. An earthquake had produced a tsunami that climbed thirty-three feet high along the northeastern coast of Japan. It caused widespread devastation, with an official count of over eighteen thousand people confirmed to be missing, and presumed killed. This was to be the highest tsunami recorded at Miyako. These happenings are always devastating and shock people around the globe every time, and yet, tsunamis have been recorded as early as 479 BCE in Greece. All structures have always been washed away and destroyed. The point here is that we need to see beyond the world in form and find the internal happiness and peace that is formless. There is no stability or promise in any structure. So where do we find stability? Stability is found in peace. Perhaps one day, maybe not in my lifetime here on earth, we will see attorneys and judges relinquish the illusion of structure and boilerplate language in divorce documents and find entirely new ways to use old words. If they could be conscious enough, they can weave sentences together that would open hearts rather than stimulate the intellect. It would be so wonderful to see a divorce that can appeal to one's heart. That brings me to the next story.

One winter day of 2003, I was standing before the Supreme Court judge at the end of my divorce trial in regards to splitting our time with the child. This was the only time in the history of our divorce that I ever heard a Court attempt to bring heart into a situation. In the following excerpt, I share the common sense that this particular judge made on that particular day. This is taken from the Supreme Court minutes.

"The Court: It's sad that I have to make a decision on something like this that the parties can't arrange to compromise some of this and work things out. It only means to me that as the kid grows up things are going to get worse and you're going to spend your life in Family Court fighting over birthdays and holidays and he arrives late and she didn't

pick up the phone. I just hope – the two of you seem like intelligent people and I would hope that it wouldn't deteriorate into that. You're going to be tied together for at least fifteen years taking care of this little boy. And how he grows up and what his relationship is with his parents is going to determine who he is, how he succeeds and what his personality is. This is not me talking, this is every psychologist, psychiatrist in the world. The kid is going to be affected by it if he hasn't already, and it's sad to see the two of you are so stubborn about things. That's the only word I can think of. Any visitation that I tell you should go into effect, I'm going to tell you without question is going to be modified down the line. There's going to come a time when Aunt Hilda is going to die and you're going to want to go to the funeral, and somebody's birthday and Disney World is going to give a special, and God knows what's going to happen."

In my view, the judge made good sense that day. All of the fighting to win, and refusal to bend, greed, and need to control all trickles down to one person. Your child. The child has no other choice except to cope with or drown from the poor displays of discord, and the lack of honor and respect. This results in children of divorced parents experiencing a gross absence of a demonstration of love. So, the separation they are really suffering is that of love. Separation of love is far worse than the separation of form, like that of a family structure. We may not be able to avoid divorce, but we can certainly choose to do it with grace and dignity, by speaking, doing and acting out in love, to ensure generational blessings for your children and your children's children to come.

It also helps to trust in Divine timing. No matter what the circumstances, hold steadfast in that timing and know that everything will be okay. I remember one day, after a turn of events I was unable to seek help from my attorney because he had already left on holiday during this season. I couldn't go the courts because most of the judges go on holiday for the season. Getting any kind of assistance from the attorneys and courts on a Friday late afternoon before Christmas is like trying to get a kettle of water to boil in ten seconds. It is just not likely to happen. We trust that attorneys will have our back and fight for us in an instant, and we trust that the courts are readily available to protect us. The reality is, the world is driven by dates on a calendar and hands on a clock, rather than minds on the heart. Because of this, the very system and people we trust will let us down. It can't help but let us down because all things in the world of form are governed by time, which is always transient. This disappointment then spins into feelings of outrage, anger, betrayal, and fear. That trust you once had in systems and people, suddenly become a malignant disease that metastasizes your emotions, stopping your mental capacity to cope with anything peacefully. Often it will affect you physically, causing disease. I am not suggesting that people cannot be trusted and are not kind-hearted. Many can, and many are. What I am saying is that people can only be trusted at the level in which their state of consciousness lies, at that given moment in time. The lesson here is to trust in Divine timing and be at peace with it. Simply put, be okay with it and just trust it. It is that central knowing of an infinite truth that will never let you down. This trust will bring you peace and calm beyond what intellect can ever offer. Beyond the mind's understanding. It is not logic. Trust hovers above logic in a space of uncertainty that just knows all is well. This trust is the assuring truth that does not close down at night and is always available on holidays. There is no clock time in Divine

Oneness, only the present moment. Trust in it and let all expectations of the moment go. This will release the fear. Because there is no fear in Divine Oneness, only love. Trust in Divine love. It is truly the only thing that matters and can be depended upon. Instead of acting on the illusion of fear, chose to be in acceptance of what is, and trust the Universe to serve you in perfect Divine order.

Decades ago, when I was that child in the lion's den, I imagine that my father was misled by doctrine and dogma, and his interpretation of it. The Bible shows many references to the fear of God and the fear of man in both the Old and New Testaments, however, the word origin of fear in both the Greek and Hebrew language also means reverence. In my view, we should love, not fear. And under that umbrella of love comes reverence, honor, respect, and trust in the Divine. If we can do this, it can carry us through a purpose driven path that keeps us from missing the mark. Perhaps this was what my beloved father didn't get and I imagine this kind of mindset and belief system was the very thing that kept him living in fear and self-torment. I cannot speak for him or for the choices he made, but I can honor him as part of the unified field of energy in which we are all somehow connected. On a much larger unimaginable scale, if you will, we are all one. I wish I were able to talk to my father today about what I have learned. Some may say that my father would be turning in his grave from what I am writing. But I say, he is not in his grave. Perhaps the deteriorating body is, however the soul never dies. Even if you do not believe any of this, it does not stop the Universe from operating in all of its infinite wonders.

Years ago, if someone were to tell me that what I was going through was some kind of Divine design, I would have said they were nuts. I may have even gotten angry. You as the reader may be in a dark place right now, feeling defeated and let down because of your current life situation. I get it. But is it possible for you to let go of the need to understand it, and instead trust in what you do not understand? Is it possible for you to accept that which you do not understand and trust in the unknown? The truth is, uncertainty can bring great wisdom. Uncertainty is not your enemy but is an open door to the ever changing unknown, where life is constantly being renewed. At every breath. Because truly, nothing is forever and everything is for a while. Sometimes we just need to trust what we cannot see or understand. We cannot feel the earth spinning on its axis, but we trust we will not fall off. We trust that the Universe is working for us and gravity holds us here because this is what science tells us. Today, science is now recognizing that we are all connected in a unified field of energy. Spiritual teachers have been saying this for centuries. Is it possible for you to connect that link of trust which fuses the heart, and the mind together? And in that connection can you integrate it with spirit? When we can connect all three, the potential is there for the arising of deep intuitive insight, which is the wisdom in uncertainty that I speak of.

Inventor, engineer, and physicist Nikola Tesla supposedly once said, "The day science begins to study non-physical phenomena, it will make more progress in one decade than in all the previous centuries of its existence." Today, I see this already happening. More and more people are beginning to take that conscious shift from a thought-based mentality to awareness. This alert awareness puts us in presence, aligning us with the Universe. With Divine Oneness. With God. Once you have come to this level of awareness which some call enlightenment, you will begin to see a reason to celebrate every day as a holy day, because the truth is each day is a gift to be celebrated in all of its continuous renewal. Celebrate life. Not the hallmark date on a calendar. None of that really matters. It is all transient. It is all part of the form of this world that breathes impermanence. Man-made occasions put on a calendar will come and go. They will bring you temporary satisfaction or dissatisfaction. But the phenomena of nature, of the Universe, is happening in each moment in all of its infinite wisdom. These phenomenal instances are formless. No one and nothing can ever take these natural occurrences away. It is what is experienced on the basis of reality. When I speak of the basis of reality, I speak of presence. Truly, this is where infinite peace and joy emerge.

At the time in my life after this divorce, the compilation of one event after another seemed never ending. I felt as if the schemes were constantly falling from the sky like random parachutes. I later learned that nothing is random. These schemes, in fact, became my teachers that taught me invaluable lessons. Many of the occurrences I experienced seemed criminal to the heart and mind. All acts of hate are criminal no matter how you label it, and no matter what costume it wears. Any feelings other than love have the potential to manifest into acts of hate, vengeance, revenge and utter madness. The trick is mastering how to stay present in all of the madness so you don't lose yourself. I wish I had understood this sooner. It took me years to learn how to end the suffering.

If any readers are experiencing a divorce or sudden separation, I passionately suggest that you let go of the battle. The war against your ex-spouse, partner, or family member, will affect your child negatively every time unless he or she has a highly realized connection to self at a very young age. Although not impossible, I don't find that is the case in most situations. In most situations, the child is wounded during all of your marital and post-divorce wars. Understand that domestic violence includes harassment and threats via voice mail messaging, e-mails, hate letters and text messaging. Some people argue that name calling, disparagement and belittling are not abuse. However, abuse is not only physical. In my view, and that of the Coalition of Domestic Violence, diminishing verbiage and constantly being put down is very damaging to a victim and is the common behavior of an abuser. During my divorce and post-divorce experience, I received piles of hate letters. For nearly twenty years I was called everything in the vocabulary book of insults from

'incredible loser' to 'psychotic', 'damaged goods' to
'pathetic', and so on. No person should ever read words like
this with their eyes or listen to verbiage like this with their
ears. And no child should ever have to witness disparagement
of a parent. Ever. Refrain from unloving ingredients. It is a
recipe for emotional destruction for all involved.

In the past, I allowed actions and words to affect me
because I had not yet learned about the unconscious elements
of the ego, the birth of pain, and the cause for suffering.
Today, I am grateful that outrageous behavior from anyone no
longer has an effect on me. With technology these days, who
would have thought that delete was to become such a
harmless and invaluable option? The only intent in
mentioning my experiences is to empower those reading this
book who may be in an abusive relationship with either a
partner, ex-partner, spouse, ex-spouse, child, adult child,
mother, father, or sibling. Know that you have the power
within to rebuke unkind acts every time. Don't respond.
Hang up. Delete. Walk away. Wake up and do whatever it
takes to resist. Be aware that whatever you fight, you
strengthen. It is critical that you understand this. You do not
need to be prey for anyone's pain, however, be aware that

there is tremendous power in taking no action, and gracefully letting it go. Let go of any feelings of rejection, because the only rejection that is harmful is self-rejection. Stop seeking understanding and validation in others who hold their own inner selves in question. They don't know who they are, so how can they know who you are? Those who did not know or understand Jesus Christ crucified him. But Jesus remained true to who He was and what He represented. Divine Love. It sends a powerful message of how we can respond to our own crucifiers. Why in this world would you let any one's words or actions cancel you out? Take your power back. Make the choice to love yourself, and turn from self-rejection. Embrace the infinite joy within. This will help keep you in that peaceful place. Why care how someone judges you? Two simple words come to mind now when any judgment or hate comes my way from anyone. It works well because, on a much larger scale, it puts things in complete perspective. Those two words are: So what? Recognize that every judgment tossed your way is many times an act of self-judgment. Remember it has been said that whenever you point a finger at another, there are always three more fingers pointing back at you. If we saw the world as a mirror, perhaps we would do less judging and more loving. So send out love and instruct the world to mirror that love back.

According to the Coalition of Domestic Violence, there are many facets to it. Emotional, mental, financial and physical. I found that the common denominator in all domestic violence is the dishonoring. That dishonoring is what destroys relationships. When a relationship between partners, parents, children, siblings, or friends do not express honor for one another, the relationship becomes jeopardized. When a relationship is void of honor, it is void of love. It is that simple. I speak from experience and trust that any stories I have been sharing on these pages will inspire unconscious people by inviting them to look into the window of their soul and seek their own healing. Healing always begins with love. We are all capable of healing and living with love. I believe it is our birthright. But we need to choose it. We need to make the conscious choice to love.

What I learned after years of suffering in post-divorce, was that fighting unconsciousness only draws you into unconsciousness yourself. For me, this was one of the hugest lessons I learned. With this wisdom, I began to disengage as I became more and more conscious in life. Fighting the good fight took on a whole new meaning for me on a heightened spiritual level that can only be explained as presence. That presence became Oneness. Not only did I feel whole, but I knew I was a special piece of a puzzle that represented something so much bigger in this mystical map of the Universe and beyond. Knowing this brought me a sense of peace, and suddenly I saw through all of the minutiae in life situations. That said, I gained a new set of eyes that showed me the only thing that truly matters. Love.

Accept all challenges and adversities because they are how we learn, why we grow, and what helps us evolve into our higher self. I will discuss acceptance in later chapters, but for now, understand that the obstacle courses before you are meant to heighten your awareness. Not hinder it. The obstacles are there to give you the opportunity to overcome so that you can continue to grow closer toward your higher self and with a deeper level of consciousness. This doesn't mean you must jump every hurdle alone, either. When you can be connected during challenging times, you can begin to recognize little gateways of opportunity that lead you to others in life on this earth to assist. Regardless of what the dialogue in your mind may be telling you, understand that

you are not here to do it all on your own. People need each
other for love, nurture, support, guidance, and also protection.
You will find that when you have adversity, certain people
will drop into your life at significant times in order to assist
you. And then you may also notice that after the storm, they
vanish just as suddenly and gracefully as they appeared. They
can help to feed and grow you spiritually and assist in
catapulting you forward. It can be a partner, a best friend, a
colleague, a neighbor, a mentor or coach, or someone who
you just met in passing. Their purpose is to help you
remember why you are here, and sometimes to remind you of
what you are here to accomplish. They are not there to be
leaned on, as much as they are there to perhaps give you that
needed boost that sends you on your way. These connections
being so needy driven, may be relationships that are short
lived. No matter how short or long they last, understand that
these personal encounters always serve a higher or deeper
purpose. I have had a few encounters in my life experiences
that I share in this book. Perhaps this sounds somewhat
esoteric, but whether you believe it or not, does not stop you
from experiencing it. That is the beauty of the Universe. It
just is. And things happen as they are supposed to. But you

must be conscious enough to observe it and choose these opportunities intuitively. So when you are in the midst of adversity, be in acceptance and know that it is an opportunity to learn, and can also be an opportunity to meet others that will remind you who you are, and why you are here.

For all of the divorced parents reading this book, I suggest that your ultimate goal be peace and not power. Love, and not fear. Release any feelings of hate or thoughts of vengeful behavior. Any turmoil you continue to stir up, not only keeps you living in the past and out of the present moment but also prevents you and the other parent from being the ever so present care giver that your child so deservedly needs and desires. Choose your words and actions wisely. Choose them lovingly. Stop wasting your time and money in court. I love and respect my attorneys, but prefer to have laughs with them over coffee, then spend endless amounts of time and money in the courts. Stay out of court as much as possible, and spend your time exercising the love in your heart with your children. Constantly pour love on them by showing your children love through experience. Conversely, in your quest for revenge and gaining control, births a journey that can lead to your child's despair, depression, unhappiness, confusion, anxiety, and utter feelings of separation. Remember, it is not the separation of parents that I speak of, rather the separation of love. This can take years to turn around, if at all, which is why breaking the mold for generational blessings is so critical. If you are currently going through a divorce, don't just do it the best that you can. Do it the best that it can be done. And doing it the best that it can be done, means keeping the peace as your ultimate goal. Peace is to be your bull's eye. The simple things like exercising the spirit of kindness and understanding, flexibility and generosity are what will bring peace. Back then, instead of seeing peace as the ultimate goal, I chose to fight unconsciousness which only drew me into my own unconsciousness.

This was a relatively short marriage, long divorce, and relentless in its post-divorce happenings and events. Today I am grateful for all of the experiences and course of events throughout this relationship, as they were all opportunities that eventually brought me back home. When I speak of home, I speak of love.

CHAPTER 6

Behind a Veil of Silence

FEELINGS OF DIMINISHMENT, loss of power and control, and turbulent divorce proceedings were not enough pain for me. Apparently, I needed a second building to fall on my head, to have an awakening. I soon entered into another marriage, which came with a rocky territory that was completely foreign to me. My new relationship came packaged with pain and addictions that were far deeper than what I saw at surface level. It was to be the relationship that shook me, wore me and woke me. Looking back, I judged it as odd that I had two bad marriages in a row because the few relationships I had before these were extremely loving. It wasn't an attraction I had toward unconscious people. Rather it was a disconnect from self, and from my inner child that needed to be addressed before walking into a new relationship. Since relationships are teachers, it seemed there was more I needed to learn. I imagine if I were present, and had truly loved myself and joined in spiritual matrimony with my inner child, perhaps I would have made more conscious choices at that time in my life. There was healing that needed to take place, and I did not make the choice to love myself first. The healing power of self-love and how it can transform all that is was still foreign to me at this time. So instead of healing, I journeyed into a new relationship.

It was to be the marriage that would break me. Literally. It began in perceived love and ended in me running for my life and I never looked back. It took nine years of being a battered wife behind a veil of silence to take my power back, get control of my life and end the suffering. My aha moment was in the knowing that I was suffering and in my decision to make it stop. If you are sitting in a deep hole that is filling up quickly with water, do you stay there helpless with worry and suffer while waiting for the water to go over your head and drown? Or do you become conscious and see that you have options in each moment to climb, tread, swim, or do whatever it takes to get out? When I made the conscious decision to see my options in that moment without worrying about an outcome, I was able to breathe. Even in threatening waters. The second I stopped worrying about everything I was convinced might happen, and let go of whatever I thought was supposed to happen, I felt inner peace. The pain and suffering transmuted into love and joy. Once I understood that the suffering was not my truth but was an illusion, it seemed simple to release. It took years to grasp this understanding because I was living in history and anticipation, rather than the moment at hand. I wish I could have reached out to my dad, or my brothers. I didn't feel that open arm connection that I needed to extend an honest arm. Relationships were not fused together, where I felt I could open up and speak of my reality. So lived with the pain and suffered greatly. Although pain comes in many different forms in life, it is not a thing. It is an experience that can be held in or recognized and released. Suffering does not exist except in yesterday's story or tomorrow's worries. So if we can truly be tuned into the moment, we can begin to breathe through the pain without all of the suffering.

In the past, I kept trying to fix things that occurred, which always took me out of the moment. It put me in a perpetual state of non-acceptance for what was. Since childhood, I always seemed to give myself the personal burden to fix any life situations surrounding me that were broken. What I found after five decades, is that we are not here to solve the problems of the world. We are here to love and come to know the loving 'I am' within us. And when we come to know the 'I am' within us, it is all about holding onto it throughout every life circumstance. Once I understood to accept the situation around me, I was able to escape the insanity without worrying about tomorrow. Most of what I had a hard time accepting was the fact that I fell into a similar hole, larger than the one I had just climbed out from. I was ashamed and felt that I made mistakes and bad choices. Even my father told me this while I was in my darkest hour, rather than supporting me in a time of severe pain and suffering. My siblings had busy lives full of houses, businesses, vacations, friends, and family. Although I had similar things, my life cycle, on the other hand, had me drowning in emotional quick sand. I never spoke of the madness behind closed doors. I kept trying to fit into this human costume I was given from birth and the tighter it got, the closer I got to the biggest awakening of my life. At the time, all I could see in my personal circumstance was another failed marriage, and

I was refusing to accept it. That is how powerful the ego can be. Much of my feelings of denial, self-judgment, and self-blame were directly related to the years of verbiage from my previous marriage and post-divorce events. After all, by this time my mind was conditioned into believing that I was 'such an incredible loser'. When I decided to love myself and peel off the labels, I was able to receive Divine grace and dignity that was waiting for me on the other side of these catastrophic situations I saw as my life. This was my turning point. Sometimes it takes a few bad breaks before we awaken.

What I learned in all of this was that we do not make mistakes. I repeat this throughout the book because it is vital in your steps toward becoming conscious, returning to love, and sprouting like grass blades through cracks in the cement. Every mistake we have been told we've made came from the illusion that we should be fitting into this glitzy costume. The lesson here is that you have never made a mistake. Every choice that you have made up until this point was perfect, regardless of how it may seem to you. I write this with deep compassion from my heart to yours. So breathe it in. All of your life choices like the partners you choose, your choice to be single, your career choices, and every physical, emotional, mental and financial choices have all been from the view point of the soul, a remarkable service to you. Know that all is well, and everything will be okay as you journey in this schoolroom of life. I know it may not have been an easy journey for some of you readers. I understand. The fact that the discussion of an unfitting costume even comes up, is cursor if you will, pointing at the fact that you are not comfortable with what you are wearing. Your costume is not your safety net. This belief system will keep you uncomfortable your entire life, restricting you from the true expression and being that you truly are. I encourage you to remove it. Explore different ways of expressing yourself from the view point of a naked, label-free, nameless soul. Experience every moment in life and know that every moment has a choice in it. Whether you choose to bless and embrace your world or deny it, is your choice. Instead of identifying yourself as this or that in the world, realize that you *are* the world. Never allow yourself to be identified with a name or label. Truth cannot be named. You are not your social status, and you are not your bank account. You are not even your family name. What I am saying is that you are not your experience. Life is not defined by your experiences, rather your experiences bring opportunities for you to get closer to your higher self.

Stop saying your life stinks. Be in acceptance of your current situation, without judging it and without identifying with it. Don't look outside to find yourself. Your truth is not in the world. It is within you. Be present and make a conscious choice to close each experience that no longer serves you. You have lost nothing and have never failed. You are beautifully unique and are a vital piece of the Universe that is here on purpose and for a purpose. Nothing is random. Reading this page is exactly where you are supposed to be at this moment. Honor yourself for being here. Some of you readers may not believe in the spiritual ways of the Universe. That is fine. It doesn't demand that you believe in them. Lack of belief does not affect the Universe at all, or your special place in it. You will not be penalized. You will always be loved. How wonderful to know that outside of illusion, beliefs have no relevance whatsoever. Life is not affected by our beliefs, however, our beliefs do affect our lives. You may need to reflect on this for a while as I did. In the years past, I have read things similar to this statement but never quite understood it until later on in life. Because all things of form are transient, so are we as human beings. We transition from infant to toddler, and teen to adult. We gain weight, we lose weight, we get braces, and maybe we break a limb or two. We have marriages and divorces. We experience loss of loved ones and personal illnesses. We think different now as an adult than we did as a teenager. Our dreams and desires often change. The point is that we transition through life all of the time. This is a fact. Knowing and understanding this is fascinating because we can begin to view our self through a different lens. In this realization, we can create our transient self, and our experiences in a way that better serves us and others. What we believe creates our transitional self, all of the experiences we have, and all of the relationships we have as we go through life personally transitioning from one moment to the next, one year to the next, one decade to the next, and so on. We all have the ability to transform our lives, and we actually do it without even realizing it. If you can realize this now, what might you create for yourself in the now? And how would this new realization affect your life today? Perhaps you would transcend. Transcend from what? From suffering into peace. When we have true peace we have discovered happiness.

When we can feel peace no matter what the circumstance, there is no greater liberation. The goal is always to transcend.

If you are currently in a dark place, know that any fear of the future, and all of the what ifs, do not exist except in thought form. Regrets from the past are illusory. They are senseless in thought because this moment is all there ever is. When you let go of fear, love enters in. Love cannot house fear. It is just not possible. I will share just a few memoirs of this next relationship, to show how we can seemingly function in a dysfunctional environment and easily slip through the cracks of life. You may also get a sense of the depths of pain, the tragedy of sudden loss, and the feelings of rejection in an abusive and violent relationship, and yet, see the possibilities of transcending it all. I trust this will bring awareness to those who seek truth and triumph in their own life.

There were some dark moments, deep wounds, and disturbing experiences in and out of the nine years of this relationship. I chose to share the following experiences in order to show the diversity of an unconscious relationship, the unconscious actions of an abuser, and its direct effects on those who become unconscious victims. I trust it will bring a sense of self-awareness to any readers that may resonate with the following events. Each abusive relationship is darkly unique in its own way, however, as I mentioned earlier in this book, the common denominator is always the darkness.

This marital relationship was multi-faceted. In my view, my husband walked through most of the marriage unconsciously, as did I. He had a lot of pain from his past and I knew this. He also had addictions. I always felt that his real bride was Mary Jane. I knew he used marijuana to numb his mind on a regular basis, but I never knew the severity of his addiction until we moved in together. I felt it was his biggest battle, and although he had no desire to ever completely stop using, he also knew that it didn't serve him well. It seemed to me that there was an ongoing love hate relationship he had with it. He defended it and its effects as one would defend his best friend or mother. This habit grew to be the pink elephant in the room that was impossible for me to ignore after a while. He carried dusty and heavy baggage of emotional pain from his past. Although I didn't understand it until seven years into our relationship, somehow I felt compassion for him for nearly all of our years together. I suppose I had an underlying understanding that he was being driven by a force of energy that controlled him that I recognized as his inner pain. The suffering I experienced during our time together led me to that ever so common search for meaning, for answers, and for peace in my life. There seemed to be an accumulated amount of old pain that I was storing as well, which in my view through the eyes of personal experience, left me as an open target for my husband's pain to feed on. Looking back, I now know that the two past failed marriages were not failures at all. They led me to find who I am and the purpose of life itself.

If the walls could talk, they would speak of hurt and tears, but also some laughter and good loving. It appeared to me that although he loved us both very much, he seemed challenged in expressing that love regularly. In the end, I couldn't sense his love for me at all. What I came to realize in time, was that his biggest challenge was loving himself. This realization took me completely out of the story and was responsible for my own healing years later. But while I remained trapped in the story, there were many hard lessons that I learned. In the onset of this relationship, I chose to juggle many things that were in my path at the time. Raising my son, the dealings with his father in all of the post-divorce insanity, entering into this new marriage, and running three new businesses all at the same time. It was a recipe for emotional, mental, and physical overload. What I later found was that multitasking is the opposite of living a mindful and present lifestyle. One of my main focuses was my son, who was continually adjusting to his life experiences growing up with me and his step father, and that of his experiences with his biological father. I felt as his mother, it was my responsibility to show him love, security, laughter, faith, and perseverance so that when waves would wash over him, he could swim. My son was the reason I learned to stop treading the waves and swim the ocean. Till this day, I am eternally blessed with the amazing gift that my son has been in my life. I teach him to experience life in the ocean and live in that spaciousness beneath the surface.

It was a difficult plunge into peace. It came with multiple challenges. In putting an end to what was, accepting what is, and allowing for new experiences came transitional occurrences which were emotionally traumatic, and yet, life transforming.

CHAPTER 7

Power and Control

THE FIRST TIME HE HURT ME was before we were married. This was my signal to get out of the relationship but instead, I stayed in it for all of the wrong reasons. It was the night before the grand opening of my first franchise. We had a disagreement in the apartment about something which till this day I can't even recall. The only thing I do recall is that he took the hair on the back of my head in his hand and yanked my head back so fast and hard that my neck made a snapping noise as I fell to the ground. I couldn't see anything. Literally. I cried out, "I can't see." I had temporarily lost my vision for what seemed to be a few seconds. It was frightening. With fear in his voice, he ran to me, touching my cheeks as I laid on my back. I remember his voice to this day as he exclaimed with intense remorse how sorry he was. I stayed lying there in tears. He then stood up, walked over to a wall and punched it in. A few days later when he was fixing the hole in the wall I asked him, "Why did you punch the wall in?" He responded, "I thought I was going away." That was the first red light that I refused to stop at. His thoughts were justified. That kind of behavior puts people behind bars. The injury from that night brought physical adverse effects on me for years. Spine and cervical doctors said I had permanent cervical damage, and surgery was highly suggested to fix the nerve damage. I did not get the surgery and lived with numbness of the hands and fingers, neck pain, and many times was completely disabled from it. During my enlightened years, I decided to defy the doctor's verdict and have been living with it pain-free. That's a story perhaps for another book though.

One snowy cold day in New York, and I am reminded of the time my husband sent me a text while I was at work, running one of the three franchises that I owned and operated at the time. It was late afternoon. The message read: You better come home because I just threw your bird outside in the snow. Immediately, I became physically upset. It reminded me of the time when we were dating and he threw his indoor cat out because he was meowing at his bedroom door too much. The difference in concern here was that parrots cannot survive in cold weather. Any readers that have lived as a battered wife knows that an abuser will not only hurt you, but will take stabs at your heart by hurting your pets, and ultimately will escalate onto your children, if not stopped in time. I immediately called him. I asked him what was going on. He said something like this, "I told you that bringing that bird home was a mistake. Now you'll learn." He hung up. I called an employee and asked her if she could come in a little earlier, as I continued to tell her that I had an emergency I needed to tend to at home. Within an hour I was on my way home, in the snow, praying that our little parrot Pippy, was still alive. He was a green cheeked conure, approximately six inches in length and his tail added another four inches. He couldn't be more than ten inches total, including his bright red and blue feathered tail.

When I pulled into the garage, I didn't see Pippy or his large cage anywhere outside. There was a brief sigh of relief. I opened the garage door which leads into the hallway beyond the kitchen entrance. As I walked into the kitchen, my nine-year-old son was on the stool at the counter doing his homework while his step father was making him a snack. I kissed my son on the head and asked him how his day in school was. Ignoring the question, he tattled excitedly, "Daddy threw Pippy into the dishwasher." I looked at my ex-husband. He said, "He bit me." I went to the other room where we kept Pippy. He was in his cage in a complete frenzy. The top of this huge iron cage was indented. When I went to console Pippy, he was attacking me and pecking at me from his cage. My fine feathered friend was completely traumatized. Although coming out to play with us was typical, I could not take Pippy out of his cage after this event for quite a while. He would hover over the top in the rear of the cage, and if you tried to be kind to him and talk sweet to him, he would advance forward to attack, in an attempt to defend himself from future abuse. In its avian response to keep himself protected, he became detached and unapproachable for weeks. I had to regain his trust. I understood him and even honored him for protecting himself. Pippy is still alive until this day and resides with me after all these years. He has built trust with me, and I understand how abuse affects animals. With all that our cat who just passed at twenty-one years of age, and the parrot who was hatched thirteen years ago have endured and witnessed in their past environment, I honor them for the lessons I've learned by observing them. I always considered my cat to be holy. Observing how he coped and behaved, taught me plenty. In fact, I used to call him my God cat. My son always laughed at that analogy, however, I believe he understood it. There was no animal that could compare to our cat's profound intelligence and wisdom. He knew how to walk through the battle trenches and return back to those humans who expressed love. We can learn a lot from certain animals that have been put in our path. The point of this story is to confirm how abusers will always use intimidation on their victims. They will make their victims afraid by using phone texts and threats, looks, actions, and gestures. They will smash things, destroy your property and abuse your pets. It is all part of the power and control that is at the core of domestic violence.

Another example of their need for power and control is using coercion and threats. One morning after I put my son on the school bus, my husband was on a war path. Apparently, he overheard my conversation with my son before he left for school. Slipping his winter jacket through one arm and the next, I asked him to zip up. He didn't. He said he wasn't cold, and ran off onto the yellow four wheeler full of students that waited curbside our home. My husband came out from the bedroom and began degrading me and my abilities to being a firm parent. In my view, it was an issue of warmth. If he is cold he will zipper his coat. On the other hand, my husband felt that when I say something, it is to be enforced and followed out as a command. To me, it wasn't a matter of obedience and certainly not a battle worth fighting. I took pride in sending my son off to school each day in a clean and pressed school uniform, breakfast in his belly, and happy. That was my daily goal which I met every day. Creating conflict in the start of a day was not something I ever did with my son. I found it quite disturbing that the very thing I was so passionate about, like starting a day with peace was slipping further and further away from me. Many times, when the door closed behind him, my misery would begin. The differences we shared on what happened on that particular morning, which by that time was well off and running thirty minutes ago into the past, became his springboard into madness in the present. In my view, he became completely unconscious. Following me from room to room in our huge house, he yelled "I want a divorce. You better put my name on this house or I will burn this mother ******* house down!" Of course, none of this had anything to do with me or the child at the door refusing to zip his coat. I imagine it had everything to do with his fear of life.

One day he said to me, "I am going to get a younger girl pregnant and make you raise the baby. That's how you'll make up for ruining my life." That comment was a heavy blow to the heart. Not because I thought he would ever do such a thing, but because he expressed that I ruined his life. I allowed this comment to cut into me. There was so much that I felt I gave of myself in this relationship, including getting pregnant and then miscarrying as a result of him fighting with me. That's a whole other story which teaches one thing. Yelling, throwing things, and emotionally upsetting a pregnant woman leads to miscarriages. Although I knew my miscarriage was a direct result of the events of that day, I never blamed him. There was an internal knowing that the Universe had my back, and everything was happening for some perfect Divine design. After the miscarriage, he decided we should stop trying to have a baby because he had concerns that it may not be healthy for me at my age. So years later, when he threw that comment at me, I felt betrayed. I bought into those thoughts of betrayal and that brought me deeper into emotional suffering.

An abusive person is not conscious and thinks nothing of sending out emotional abuse. They will put their victim down, make them feel bad about themselves, and call them names. What's worse is that they work overtime trying to convince you that you are the crazy one. They do this by playing mind games. Abusers are also masters at blaming. After they've been violent, and have battered you to the point of losing mobility of a shoulder, neck or arm, they will blame you. "You did this. You did this to yourself", he would say.

I never heard my husband tell me that he was sorry. Not for nine years, except for that one day when he snapped my neck and thought it blinded me. I never had makeup sex either. You only see that in the movies. It is not reality, however. At least it was not my reality. His way of trying to make things right with me and himself was in trying to help me cope. Although well meaning, it is still complete dysfunction. After this one horrific occurrence, he helped me shower for weeks. As I held my one arm that was attached to my injured shoulder up over my head with my other good arm, he would wash me. This may sound romantic to you, but believe me when I tell you that there is a profound difference between your husbands caring for you because you had a ski accident, or helping because he nearly killed you. There is nothing romantic about the latter.

One November morning, days after that same occurrence, I was sitting in the kitchen sipping hot coffee with a collapsed shoulder contemplating where my life has brought me, and where I need to get it to. He walked into the kitchen and looked at me. It was evident that I was in serious pain. He said in disgust, "It makes me sick to see you like this." Was I to feel guilty that my pain was reminding him of his behavior days prior? Was it all my fault in his eyes? In my view, it seemed crazy that he could only see my physical pain and suffering. I found it to be nothing other than pure insanity. One thing I did know. This was unconscious living. Just as crazy, was the level of unconsciousness it brought me into. I withheld the truth from everyone including the doctors when I was in need of medical assistance. Before heading to a doctor, with worry he said something like, "What are you going to say? You can't tell them what happened. Are you crazy?" What came to my immediate memory was that night

so many years prior when he thought he was 'going away'.
So in turn, I told the doctor I fell off of a ladder. Wonderful, I
thought. Now fear has completely taken over and a lie will
keep me safe. How ridiculous. One day the doctor replied,
"You sure do have a lot of accidents." I'll never forget that
comment, and how it made me feel. Abusers will force you to
lie because they instill so much fear in their victim. I just
couldn't see clearly anymore. Truth clouded over me, and
only the falsehood of the relationship had prevailed,
independent of me as the observer. It was as if my spirit was
no longer breathing in this human body I was living in. It was
a very dark and lonely place.

When the violence was at its worst, where it was more
frequent than not, I experienced a beating in which I will
never forget and chose it to be my last. Phew! There are
twelve serious beatings that I journaled and still have a vivid
memory of them all. They don't haunt me anymore, although
they used to. Once I was enlightened, I was able to
completely let them go. I recognize these happenings and
events as my teachers. Every experience I had, helped
transform my life to where it is today and has brought me
back to wholeness again. I only mention this to point out that

when it becomes so frequent, the abuser is so conditioned to this behavior that they often tend to make light of the abuse. They not only dismiss your concerns and the consequences of their actions, but they actually say that the abuse didn't happen. They lie and believe their own lies. They are completely out of their mind. No one in a conscious state of mind would behave in such a manner. It is just not possible. Understanding this, however, does not free you from it. It allows you to forgive, but you will also need to take affirmative action toward your personal freedom. Sometimes you will need to tell an unconscious person to back off, emphatically, and run for your life. Literally. That is what I finally did.

If any of this sounds familiar to you, then you need an exit plan. You need it now. First, you need to know that there is no end of the tunnel. Stop waiting for it. The time is now. The light awaits you now. There is no promise of tomorrow. Forget what society and doctrine have taught you. Trust in today. Tomorrow, you or your loved one may be dead. It took me nine years to pick up the phone and call someone. That was the day I took my power and control back. I celebrate that beating which almost took my life, as a day of triumph. The date is highlighted in my mind's calendar as the day I chose freedom, and love for myself. I used that final beating as a gateway leading me back toward grace and dignity.

CHAPTER 8

How Death Became Life

IN MY LIFE SITUATION, which differs from others, of
course, I prayed for God to save this marriage. I also feared
God, because that is what I was taught by my father and in
my view, man's over-all misinterpretation of the Bible. I
believed it was my duty to stay and survive it and wait on
God to fix, heal and cure the marriage. I feared to hurt my
son and to disrupt the life he identified with. I immersed
myself in Holy Scripture and prayed on my knees day in and
day out. The final beating that I spoke of in the previous
chapter has an interesting prelude that I feel is worth telling.

It was springtime, on a Friday morning. I cried out
loud on the shower floor with my face down as the hot drops
of water streamed over me. That morning, I changed my
prayer though. I cried out for God to bring me peace within

my walls, even if that meant my death. I no longer prayed for the marriage. I just wanted to die. As crazy as this sounds, I imagined at the time that maybe if I had a terminal disease, I would get sick and die and would no longer have to suffer. This mind set was uncharacteristic of me, which tells you how low I had to get before the light switched on inside my soul. Just two days later, that Sunday I found myself beaten and being suffocated on the bed by my husband. When I could no longer put up a physical fight, I laid there in full acceptance. I gave up. At what seemed to be my final breath, my husband was holding his two hands tight around both sides of my throat and jaw. I closed my eyes and imagined my son's face, as my eyes rolled back into my head and waited for my death. There was a vivid recollection of my mind and spirit pleading, but my body remained unmoved and still, as my heart began reaching its final beat. At that moment, he slowly released his hands from my throat and jaw and fled the room. I began to breathe slowly again. My jaw was locked in one position. I couldn't move it. The Universe plucked him out of my life on that day. After the trauma, only three days later, a peace came over me and my household that was indescribable. I can only describe it as conscious presence. I found death before it found me. What I learned is that God is not to be feared. We are not life time patients in a mystical waiting room with some number attached to us. We are part of the same Divine Oneness that has always been there. We have just forgotten this because of all the madness in this human experience on earth we call life. Most of us have been taught to fear. That said, most of us have also been taught to trust fear and to use it as a defense mechanism. That's nuts. Why would anyone trust an illusion? I say to trust love, and use it as your source. Once you remember where home is, and let go of all fear, the only thing left is love. In that space, everything that is real becomes clear. And that is the knowing where nothing else exists. Only the love in that moment. The peace I gained within my walls was the peace within *my* walls. It was the re-birth of my truth. The death I gained was the death of the ego, which was really the part of my thinking mind that had been hovering over the unconscious me who I identified with. All of the things my unconscious ego was relating to, I set free. This meant letting go of my identity as a battered wife, and the warped sense of societal and doctrinal duty to fulfill. This also meant letting go of all shame for past mistakes I judged myself as making.

Lastly, this meant letting go of all fear for the future, and abolishing all of the 'what ifs'. Ego and that thought based mentality no longer ran my life. It's not that ego is bad, but that it can be very unconscious. Once I set those unconscious thoughts free, there was a clearness if you will. Like a perineal, the old unconscious ego seemed to die and a new, more conscious one had sprung up. Was ego responsible for all of my mistakes? It doesn't really matter. What matters is knowing that I made no mistakes. Every decision I made is exactly what I needed in order to recognize and embrace my true essence. My truth. Religion didn't save me. Doctrine confused me. And fear nearly destroyed me. Once you truly understand this, the death you will seek is the death of the illusory you. The illusory you is that false sense of self you have been believing that whispers, "This is who I am and this is my sad fate." This could not be further from your truth. Let go of the illusory you. Finding your truth is the birth of your triumph.

I was told that my ex-husband went on attempting to re-establish a relationship with God within the walls of a Church, as many people do when they've hit rock bottom. The problem is that broken people look outward for God, instead of inward. They imagine they are seeking inward, but they are not. They see God in a book or in a building labeled Church, Synagogue, Mosque, or Temple. Truly, you are the temple of God, and that temple is to be honored and loved. Redemption is not found in a building, it is found in self. It is found in dying to self which I discuss in various pages of this book. When someone is abusive and violent, their soul is frightened and weak. They begin to lose control of their victim, and many times hit rock bottom as all that they loved in this world of form disappear. Many times when this happens they seek some kind of redemption from some God in the heavens. I've seen this pattern in many that hit rock bottom. But the reality is that their rock bottom always has a trap door. Every abuser and every addict have one. Do not believe otherwise. The only thing that can stop them from entering into that trap door, is their own awakening. Their coming into consciousness. Supporting and coping with them, although well-meaning is not going to change them. It may even enable them. They must be personally ready to wake up and take the shift on their own.

My characteristics leaned on the side of faith and forgiveness, and I raised my son in this way. This brought more road blocks and challenges. I battled with how to respond to my son who was hurting with this immediate turn of events, as it was such a swift loss. For all three of us. One day we were a family and the next day after I was nearly killed, and he was arrested. With black bruises up and down my thighs and a locked jaw, I filed for divorce and never looked back. We never saw him again. One day my son went to our Church with his friend's family and saw his step father in the vestibule. I was told that they embraced and spoke. I never knew what was said because I was not there. That evening, I remember my son telling me in tears, that if I couldn't take him back, and if I didn't believe he could change, then every-thing I taught him about Jesus was a lie. This destroyed me, emotionally. These are the belief systems of doctrine that twist and torment us into confusion and lament in our hearts with great feelings of loss and betrayal, emotional pain and suffering. In my view, the teachings of Christ and the law of the Jews are often misunderstood as to how this all applies to our personal lives, and the world we live in today. I had to explain to my son that it is because of Christ's teachings that I *can* forgive him. I told him that we can pray for him, and even love him as a child of God, but that I could not have him back. There were so many teachings and scriptures on for-giveness that were turning with emotion inside my head. But what arose most in my mind was the fact that my husband was breaking down my body and no longer honored me. So the scripture that innately came out of my mouth was a teach-ing from the Book of 1 Corinthians in the Bible that talks about our bodies being the temple of God. I explained as I showed him scripture in the Holy Bible. He listened, but he did not appear to be buying what I was selling. After all, Christ's teachings of forgiveness are all over the New Testa-ment. But no one really defines how scripture applies to abuse, where to draw the line, and what forgiveness really means. In my view, it's because they don't really understand it themselves. I find this topic in the churches to be largely ignored, mostly because it is so misunderstood. But because this was my experience, I did understand it. And so I was confident in my answer to my son.

My girlfriend on the other hand, who was there at the time, added to the conversation quite differently. As she forked Chinese vegetable dumplings from takeout containers and onto my son's plate she called him by name sternly and said, "Hitting is a deal breaker." That sentence seemed to silence my son. It also silenced me, as I sat there with bruised skin and a bruised heart. Those five words were the real lesson, and I found to be the perfect answer. There was no further discussion about it that evening. We need to teach our children experience and not language, which I learned soon after. I then took my son to the coalition of domestic violence for counseling from someone considered an expert in the field. The goal at the time was for my son to learn the statistics of an abuser, even if they seem convicted and want to change. I remember asking the counselor privately, "How many change?" He responded in less than a second, "Five percent. The other ninety-five percent want to change, but they just can't." I went on to ask, "It's in their DNA, isn't it?" He responded, "I believe it is. Yes." It wasn't long after that my son's heart began healing, and that experience taught him a lesson that I trust will stay with him as he walks his own path in life. As difficult as it all was, this was needed in order to break the mold so that generational blessings can begin to unfold. We must always return to love, in all circumstances. That love begins with self. There is an intrinsic connection between self and God. I describe it as Divine Oneness.

I will abbreviate the rest of my journey so that those readers who question the domestic violence in their own life, or that of another can see the severity of it. Lamps were broken. Punched in walls. Twelve punched in doors. Storm doors ripped off their frames. Sliding screen doors were thrown to the in-ground pool. Glasses, cups, and bowls put in flight. Work papers flying everywhere. Toys tossed to the curb. Wind shields punched and shattered. Cabinets dented. Glass table tops smashed numerously. As for me physically, I experienced blows to my head, a concussion, black eye, severe bruising up and down my legs and arms, cervical damage, and lock jaw. There was strangulation many times, and I remember every place that each beating occurred. It lingered through the walls. This insanity weaved in and out of nine years, with the last four years at its worse. The good news is that most of these occurrences happened when my son was not home. That said, I spent much of my time scurrying around fixing things and paying people to replace things over the weekend before my son would return home. Then there were the daily ins and outs of running the business. I never seemed to be able to catch up to myself. And so, I sunk deeper and deeper into my own misery. The bad news is that the last two years of our marriage were tumultuous, and my son witnessed violence from wind shields being cracked to punching down doors and walls, to strangling me on the hallway floor. There was also a terrible altercation the morning after my sister's fiftieth birthday party. He consumed a lot of alcohol the evening of the party. The next morning when he woke he was on another war path. But this one seemed different. Looking back, I realize now that it was the after effects of all of the alcohol he consumed the night before. I imagine he may have still been drunk. It seemed to keep him in a state of belligerence and outlandish anger. He began badgering my son about a school project as he spun out of control. In defending my son from harm's way, his bedroom door wound up kicked in, and I was thrown down and strangled in the hallway. There was nothing I wouldn't do to protect my son. And my son knew this. This made my husband angrier.

After it all, I recall holding my son in my arms in his bedroom. We were sitting alone on the bed together. I whispered, "Mommy is going to make things better. I promise." We had a short and deep conversation. I read his heart and he acknowledged its accuracy. It was a sad moment. He nodded and huddled under the pit of my arm as I caressed his forehead. I kept my promise. The time and space between volatile acts became closer and closer together until about two months later on that Sunday in May of 2010. That was the day I ran for my life. My son was such a brave boy and till this day I am so amazed at how he came to my rescue in a cautious, and conscious demeanor. He handled things perfectly, in his understanding of his step father's need to be right, and his overall unconscious mental state. The ugly details of this time need no telling. Although dramatic, none of it is important. What is important is the actions we take in situations. My son responding to my scream for help, and my reaching out to the authorities is why I am alive today. Having said that, there are tens of thousands that come out of domestic violence situations carried out in a body bag.

"A Massacre Scene in a Community where Homicide is virtually Unheard of." This was a late night report, 11 pm one recent night from North Arlington, NJ. A woman found dead in her Bergen County apartment and prosecutors said that it was an apparent victim of domestic violence. Domestic Violence has become an epidemic. As a successful entrepreneur and mother, living in an affluent quiet suburban

town living behind a veil of silence, this headline disturbed me. As I have shared in this book, it took me nine years to run for my life. The point is, that behind the silent walls of "nice" neighborhoods hide the tragic acts of domestic violence. Sadly, because there is not enough awareness and education out there, people get shocked when it suddenly ends in death...a homicide. But there is nothing sudden about it. No batterer decides to just be violent one day and murder. It's years and years of abusing and controlling someone. It takes years before most battered women call the police, while others never call the police...until they are dead and on the front headline of the News. Statistics show that the number of American troops killed in Afghanistan and Iraq during 2001 and 2012 is 6,488. The number of American women who were murdered in the US by current or ex-partners during that same time is 11,766. That's almost double the casualties than in war. This number is growing. I don't need to tell you, you only have to turn on the news each day and see it. By sharing some of my stories and insight, I trust that one day they'll be an epidemic of love, and as a global community, break the mold for generational blessings.

The marriage was an amazing journey. I do not wish to revisit this path, but none the less it was a lesson that was all my own in the teaching, and am grateful that I came out alive. I used to say that I wasted fourteen years of my life in two bad marriages, but now I see it all for its amazing gifts. I may not have seen it as I was crawling through the trenches, but what a beautiful doorway that was lit up for me, in all of its magnificence when I was ready to enter. As life for me remains purpose driven, it is always in love and acceptance for what is, that brings me home. Truly, each breath is an awakening into the next. Each day is a new gift, and I will never look fear in the eyes again. I am not saying I will never feel fear, but I know for sure that I will never believe it.

"Experiences can be gateways that lead you back toward grace and dignity."

~Lily Sanders

CHAPTER 9

What Drives Someone to Violence

MANY PEOPLE HAVE ASKED ME what drives someone to violence, particularly a spouse or partner. In my own experience, both people had their own characteristics which were unique to themselves. That said, one person cannot be compared with another. As far as the topic of domestic violence, the language we have been taught since birth has clouded the truth for generations upon generations. I would like to clear up the misconceptions that most have learned growing up, and as adults have grossly latched onto these beliefs as truth. I answer this curious question confidently, as I have come to discover it in the schoolroom of life through experience and not vocabulary. The belief system tells you it takes two to tango. In truth, it does not. In my human experience, what I have learned is that most unconscious humans operate as computers. When the system malfunctions or runs slow, we either blame the internet service or fear that we have a virus or may crash. We never see ourselves beyond the hardware and the software. We hook up, we download, we upload, we store data, we delete data, we back up files, and then one day we just crash. When this happens to someone who has very heavy emotional pain from past experiences, he or she will take down everything and everyone with them. All of the things that seemed important and critical in life vanish and not a single loving person in their world can reboot them. Everything that has been stored in his or her brain eventually crash, and the entire way down they blame, accuse, misuse, abuse, and torment the very person that has loved them all along. This may be the cause of many people's addictions to alcohol, drugs, sex, pornography, violence, obsessive behavior and so on. They are all forms used to mask the pain. The problem is that it will only numb the pain temporarily, and yet the rubber band effect becomes far worse. Once they snap back to a more conscious state of mind, they don't know how to be there because they're so identified with this pain. The ego keeps telling them they are in danger, and so they keep up the addictions, and the bouts of anger and violence become heightened. They need no reason or provoking from their victim to be angry or act out in violence. They have plenty of reason all on their own, wrapped up in a painful package in their mind called pandemonium. When a person is running on just their brain, where their thoughts have become their master, they behave as a crashing computer does. They see no other choice because they are not hooked up to the main server. They have forgotten the Source in which they have come into this world from. Our body was designed to honor love, so much so that the very doorway from Divine Oneness into this physical world on earth is created by physical love. It is the only way to get here. The truth is, our bodies are programmed in the womb, before the mind ever touches them, and before society adjusts the bodies to its own fearful conditioned mind patterns. This is why I mention earlier in this book that we need to connect the heart, intuition, and the brain. And yes, our bodies are designed to dance. But they are designed to dance with the love and lightness that allows joy to enter. Dance is supposed to bring you joy. Anything other than this is not love. So when one says it takes two to tango, perhaps it can take on a different meaning and be seen in a positively different light. The tango is a walking dance of elegance, where a man embraces a woman. The embrace is never broken. They improvise in each step as the emotions from the melody and rhythm of the music overcome them. Emotion is what is shared between man and woman in the embrace. Without emotion, dancers are just, well, going through the motions where it is mere choreography to music sandwiched together. The point is, the source of dance should always be driven by the heart. By emotion felt from within and from the music. In tango, it is said that the music is the source of the emotion and the embrace is the catalyst for sharing it. That said, perhaps we can say that our connection with Divine Oneness is the source and our self-love is the catalyst for sharing it.

Another belief taught in society today is that the victim and their abuser are turned on by makeup sex. This is another gross misconception. For most of my marriage, I never turned my husband down for sex. The joy in it was gone, however. Here is the only analogy that comes to pen: You are served lamb chops all year and really enjoy the taste, the quality, and tenderness. Then one day you see the chef out back. He slaughters the little young intelligent lamb by stunning it. The method of stunning for the slaughtering of lambs and sheep is done worldwide. It involves the use of electric paddles placed on the animal's head, a shock is given which results in convulsions in the lamb, and subsequently becomes unconscious, which is by no means effective or humane. There is no sense of love present in this act, whatsoever. Next, you see the chef slit its throat open in order to sever the arteries and the animal is bled out. An hour later, the chef comes in with this beautifully cooked lamb chop on a dish. Would you want to partake of it?

What I learned through experience is that the continuum of unloving acts in a relationship creates a gulf between the two, and the physical loving that was once there can no longer exist. It cannot exist because physical loving is always an expression that honors love. You cannot hit and name call one minute, and expect to be on cloud nine with that same person a few hours later. The very idea of that is pure madness. What I found is that this deranged thinking is not only a complete disconnect from self, but is also a form of undiagnosed mental illness in many abusers. Love does not have a beginning and an end. It is not an act of doing that only takes place in the bedroom on command. Love is a state of being. When you honor love, it will follow through to a physical loving. When that relationship is void of honor outside of the bedroom, love making becomes less desirable, and in my experience has never been used as a makeup tactic. Conversely, when an intimate connection is there, it should be a place where neither is afraid to be who they are in their own body. That is why true physical loving is so euphoric. There is a beautiful harmony that is experienced. A connected-ness that needs no words. It can be enjoyed at a deeper level that involves no thought. So when you move into your physical dance or tango with your partner and experience your physical loving, remember as you remove your clothing, to remove your mind as well.

The third misconception is that people stay with their abuser because deep down, they want to suffer. The truth is, they stay because they are afraid. They are still believing fear. They fear for their physical mortality and that of their loved ones. They fear losing everything and perhaps being in hiding in some shelter for victims. However, at a much deeper level, they also fear their own evolution. They believe what they are being told by their abuser and others, and they believe their own negative thoughts as well. They have not recognized these fears as an illusion, which is all they ever are. They are not yet ready for the shift, from thought into awareness. Ego still has a firm grasp on them. Additionally, a battered person is typically alienated from family and friends, or have mastered the secret so well that it becomes extremely challenging in their reaching out for help. Especially when in an affluent environment. Who will ever believe them? This is what fear tells them. So they go on living behind a veil of silence until they can no longer stand the suffering, or perhaps are found dead and on the front headlines of the News.

Conversely, when a person is ready for the shift into awareness and remembrance of love, that awakening will birth an intense sense of peace. This was my personal experience and very much the motivation in writing this book. I honor my past pain as teachers in this life and know that in sharing these stories, others can learn from it and apply some of these insights to their own unique situations. Remember, it is not the added story we are relating to. However, the commonality in how our own unique pains around the globe at whatever intensity they may be, are all reminders that pain is not our individual burden.

Remember, you are not your experiences, rather your experiences are part of your life situations that have the potential to help you grow. Your experiences are as transient as the wind. Imagine that you are in a space or magnetic energy field surrounding your situation. Use that powerful wind to rise up and soar above all life situations. The recognition of this deeper sense of formless being can help you discover the very essence of you, which will always bring you back home. When I speak of home, I speak of love.

CHAPTER 10

The Cost of Rage

PEOPLE SAY IT'S TOO HARD TO LOVE. I say it is too painful not to. This is because our intrinsic nature is love. Love is the fundamental essence of who we are. Anything that is not aligned with our true nature is going to have a difficult time dwelling there. Love cannot house hate. During my personal awakening, I was married to an unconscious man with a lot of old and new pain that had taken over his life. I was a mere punching bag living under the same roof. We started losing a lot of income, and all of my retirement funds had dwindled to nothing. He became the unpredictable turbulence whose mind easily evaporated at normal temperatures, and when the heat of life's circumstances was raised, he was set aflame. The world blames unloving acts on stress, and

lack of financial freedom. It is much deeper than this, however. The stress and lack of finances is a trigger, but not the
culprit. When someone is unhappy and has lost their ability
to love, it doesn't matter if they are rich or poor. Until they
find the love of self, they can never really be happy. This was
a pivotal time for me as I began to come more and more into
presence. I remember my love for self and for life bothering
him so much that in his observation of me waking up and re-
tiring at night happy, was utterly and undeniably disturbing to
him. One morning I recall him saying to me in the kitchen,
"How can you walk around happy all the time as if everything
is just fine?" I looked at him with compassion. I told him
that my happiness comes from within. My response sparked
him and he walked away talking to himself out loud. I
watched him in complete conversation with himself, asking
and answering all of his own questions. Having witnessed
this before, I hoped it might help him figure things out. This
never happened, but it was still a better option than violence.

The temper tantrums, on the other hand, came out of
left field. I remember one day he was on his way to take a
course in community college and I was on my way to work at
our place of business. As he exited the front entry way, the

inconsistent handle of the storm door finally broke as he turned it. His face heated up as he ripped the entire storm door off its frame and we watched it dangling on its hinges. The mental meltdown overcame him. He was as temperamental as the door handle. I felt as if I was standing with a mentally insane patient who had just escaped the psych ward of a hospital. I looked at him calmly and said, "Go to class. I will fix the door. Go." I saw fear in his eyes, as the eruption of his violence silenced him. He scurried down the driveway into the car. The wheels of the car spun off at the same speed of the wheels in his mind. I called my employee and asked if she could stay an hour longer. I got my tools and dismantled the broken storm door off the molding. I remember dragging the ruins to the curb and thinking…what the heck has my life come to? How am I ever going to escape these short tempered people that keep entering my life and gradually bleeding me out? Why is this happening? These were the days I began searching within for real answers.

Another day, my son broke his front tooth playing in the house with his friend. My husband was so upset that he broke his front tooth and ranted on about it. The rage in him began thrusting all of his toys out to the curb. His volume raised as he communicated how he couldn't understand why a boy with a room full of toys could play with a ball in the house and get hurt, instead of playing with his toys in his playroom. I imagine in his view, he felt he was making a point of this by throwing half of his toys to the curb in front of me, my son, and his friend. It was a complete moment of insanity.

One morning, after my son went off on the school bus I made my usual cup of coffee and began doing all of the bills for the business and placing orders for things. I could hear the birds' morning songs outside the window as I enjoyed the morning ritual of presence just sipping on coffee. All of my papers were piled in order, out and about the long kitchen counter. Suddenly, I heard the tone of my husband's foot-steps get louder as he came out of the master bedroom, across the catwalk and down the staircase. The pace and sound of his steps alerted my senses and I imagined he woke with a disturbed heart. He entered the kitchen and asked me a ques-tion. I was unable to answer his question with certainty in that moment and paused. The chirping birds, the warm cof-fee, the piled papers…none of which had any nexus to his question. I switched mental gears and began contemplating the answer to his question. "Why do you take so long to answer a question? Is there something wrong with you?" he howled. I recall looking up at him and wondering how someone could wake up so miserable. His body got heated as he swooshed his hands across the kitchen counter sending all of the once organized paper work in flight like the birds, along with the coffee cup that shattered onto the floor.

The point here is that the more conscious I became the angrier he got. When someone is quick to anger and wakes up disturbed, it is typically based on fear. People who are said to be mean spirited, are actually frightened individuals. They act out with rage because they live in fear. When you live in fear, you are pushing love further and further away. It is so paralyzing that you forget how to walk in love. It was a process for me personally, to let go of my fears but was well worth it. Once I was able to let go of my own fears and see the loving things in life, I noticed that the fear in my husband, which I will call pain could not tolerate the love in me. Our differences in the level of consciousness separated us greatly toward the last few years of marriage. Sometimes we can be helpful in bringing someone to the light, and sometimes they simply are not ready to evolve. In our situation, it was the latter. In all that transpired in the name of fear and anger, what did it cost to carry this rage? In my view, it cost his marriage, his role as a step-father, and all that he identified himself with at that time in life. I know he loved us both very much, and I imagine he was challenged in expressing that love because he had so much past pain.

If you are reading this book and can resonate to any of this behavior, I encourage you to ask yourself the same question. What has rage cost you? If you are currently experiencing a situation that you are feeling rage from, see if it is possible for you to set the situation down before you, and say "I no longer want you in my life. I no longer want this pain." If you are hurting, see if you can tell yourself, "I am hurting. But I am okay." Here again, is an opportunity for self-investigation or self-inquiry which can bring tremendous inner growth. In order to do this, you will need to go to the heart and listen to it intently. Ignore the mind. The mind wants you to believe what it is telling you. Don't believe it. Truth is in your heart. Ask your heart what your truth is, and what it is doing for you in this moment. Your heart will always speak the truth. It will always speak the truth in love.

Listen to it. It will bring a sense of peace and calm. Everyone has the opportunity to awaken and find the light within. We may have loving people around us that send love, however, the key to our true happiness is found within. Only you hold the key to your heart. In my view, when it comes to relationships it isn't anyone's position to fix or save another. We are not here to solve the world's problems. You may have purposed yourself to solve certain things in the world. But in truth, we do not have to solve life, nor do we need to fear life. We are only here to love and become complete as we navigate through life situations. The Universe will take care of the rest. The key is to love, and not fear. And the way to evolve is through love.

"People say it's too hard to love. I say it's too painful not to."

~Lily Sanders

CHAPTER 11

The Dimensions of Loss and Growth

IT WAS NEARLY TWO MONTHS AFTER my husband was arrested. As difficult as it was to transition through this sudden life change without ever wavering or looking back, it was exactly what my heart was telling me and instinct knew that everything and everyone would be okay and grow enormously from this. At this point, I knew that I was here to express love and not to be a victim of another person's pain. I knew the same for my son. As deep as the suffering was with the breakup of our family unit, I found that what we really grieved was the finality of any hope that we had as a family. It was devastating because all our hearts were shattered. The idea of love and that forever family unit was now gone. It was all an illusion. The only thing that remained standing amongst the rubble was the present moment. Everything else was demolished right before our eyes. I struggled to understand it for a while and later came to realize that these changes were necessary for the evolution that was awaiting. What I didn't know was how deep the loss would feel before feeling any sense of peace. There is an enormous amount of loss and separation experienced in a sudden divorce, and just as in death, each loss is experienced in its own unique way. Loss is loss. I believe that all losses are necessary. We may not welcome them. But they are necessary for self-growth.

I cried some nights for the loss of him in my life. Not for me, or my son for that matter. But for him. Deep down, I knew he was stuck in this abyss of pain that caused him to act out unlovingly. He was the one human whose soul I could sometimes see into. Not in an angelic way, but in a tortured, reaching way that encompassed a broad range of emotions, fear, and pain. In my view, it is what drove him to his addictions which are no different than any of us, really. The problem with addictions is that one will do anything to have, use, or obsess over something at all costs. Addictions are like tattoos. You can't just have one. You become obsessed, and before you know it, you are a slave to your mind where spirit becomes so far removed. The passion for addictions obscures the love for self. For nine years I wanted nothing more than to see him over-ride that force that seemed to control his mind. What I learned is that everyone gets glimpses of light, wake up calls, and nudges from spirit. Love is not prejudiced. No one is left out. We all get chances to awaken. But it is up to each individual's choice to choose love. And when you choose love, you can return home. When I speak of home I speak of the natural essence of who you are. That natural essence is light, love, and oneness. What I found is that sometimes we need to travel through dimensions of loss and growth in order to get home.

The Catwalk

At my husband's arraignment, there was a stay away order of protection put into place, and the detectives put a panic alarm in our home behind my bed. There were twenty-five panic alarms that were given to the police department to service all of two counties with two million, eight hundred and forty-nine thousand people in it. One of them was graciously given to me. If he went against the order and entered the home or property, I would press the panic button which would bypass central station and go directly to the police cars that were nearby. This was a high alert protection system which meant they would drop their coffee and run. One of the reasons I stayed in this battered situation for so long was because I thought I would never be protected properly and he would come back and kill me. I remember many times thinking in my mind that I would be found dead in a dumpster and my son would have no mother. This was not a healthy place to be. That is how powerful the mind is. It is equally debilitating when you buy into what others tell you, and what society tells you through the media, propaganda, film, and television. I find this kind of mind conditioning to be responsible for most of the worry, disease, and madness in the world today. Having this form of protection given to me, which I never knew existed, was one example of how my fear and worry, and all of the 'what if's' had no power over the truth.

My husband was to arrange for a police escort in order to come into the home for his things. Instead, he made arrangements with one of my brothers to have some of his clothes and personal belongings picked up somewhere outside the home. This was agreed upon because none of us wanted my son to be exposed to any more than he had already been exposed to. As for me, I was unable to even look at him, no less see him come into the home with a police escort to get his things. Bruised and traumatized after the assault, the thought of him anywhere near me was utterly frightening. Additionally, I was committed to never looking back. That meant never giving him a moment, an inch, or opportunity to turn that around. Absence without fail is the sure way to stay safe, and remain focused on a new life of peace and love. That is why these orders of protection are given to victims by the courts. They should always be abided by, and a victim should never waiver. Ever. You will need to remain steadfast in your decision to dissolve the relationship. Your complete absence will send a clear message to the abuser that it is over. In order to gain back love, grace, and dignity for yourself, you must continue to choose it for yourself. Don't waver, and don't entertain any third party communication from your abuser. You don't owe him or her anything. The only thing you owe is love for self. The only attention you are to give is to yourself and your children.

I gave bags of his things to my brother and off he went. It was later in the evening. The street lights dimly lit the curbside. My brother had his things and waited outside in the street in front, but away from the house for him to arrive. There was a big square window above the front entrance door of the home. You could see out to the street through that window from inside the house, depending on where you were situated on the catwalk. I remember me and my son sitting in the dark, in the middle of the catwalk on the floor. We held onto each other and looked in between the wrought iron banister as we watched them through the big square window. We observed them exchanging words and bags of clothes were handed to him. My brother began walking off the street and toward the house again. I told my son to stay on the catwalk, and I went down to the door and let my brother in. He said that my husband wanted a bag that was in the front closet tucked away on the top shelf. I went to the front closet, found the bag in question, and gave it to my brother to bring out to him. In the clear bag was a pipe, a lighter, and his friend Mary Jane. After all that had transpired, I imagined that his yearning for numbness was heightened. Since all that he had was no longer, it seemed to me that the pink elephant in the room remained to be his best friend and 'go to' antidote. My brother and I looked at the bag, then at each other. He put the bag in his jacket and out of view from my little boy. Scurrying back out, across the lawn and back to the street he went. It was comforting to watch the pink elephant walk out the front door. It was like watching the other woman finally leave the household. Walking back up the steps, I re-joined my son on the catwalk. We watched again in the dark distance as he handed the bag to him. We could see that there were words exchanged, then a short embrace, and then off he went slowly with his chin low. Suddenly tears began to stampede down our cheeks. It was a speechless moment of sudden loss, and tears overwhelmed us as they flooded the catwalk. There were a lot of unspoken emotions that came with this loss, and they all connected to the one thing. Pain. In that moment I sensed that we felt each other's pain. We said nothing. We didn't need to. There was a silent knowing that we shared, and because of that, we were able to experience a shared compassion and love toward each other. It seemed to lessen the suffering for the moment. I carried my little boy to his bedroom, tucked him in and lied beside him until he fell asleep. I remember massaging his arms and hands, as I often did at night to help ease any tension from the day, and to help him fall asleep peacefully. As I did this, I recall his little hands reminding me of when I used to admire them all of those years before when he was just an infant. Time had passed, our bodies had grown and transformed, and yet it seemed like yesterday that he was that tiny infant nursing on my lap. I was beginning to realize how even we, as human beings, are transient.

Because of this, it is so important to make each transient moment in life count. For that of your own experiences and that of your children's. This means taking into account the only thing that matters. Love. How many children need their hearts broken before we wake up to the only thing that matters? When will we begin to see a collective conscious choice to express love in all relationships? Be aware of what you say to a spouse, a child, or in the presence of a child. Take responsibility for your actions to a spouse or a child or a parent. If you feel incapable of expressing love, walk away. Be silent. Do whatever it takes to resist the wars of the ego. You can always revisit a situation if you still feel it is necessary after you have been able to do your internal work. It all boils down to the one thing. Letting go of the trash that is collected in your mind and choosing to love. As parents, we will never be able to stop our children from feeling pain at one level or another. Nor would we want to. Because everyone must experience pain in order to have the opportunity to evolve. It has been said that pain is built into our biology. But what we can do for our children, is alleviate their suffering by teaching them how to guard their thoughts. Because suffering is more mental and thought provoking. I discuss this in later chapters.

All children really want is love. For that matter, it is all any of us really want. This doesn't mean saying I love you in the morning and I love you at night seals the deal. Although well-meaning and sincere, we need to go much deeper than surface level. We need to teach beyond language. We must teach them what love is through experience. So as they grow up in their own little costume that begins to get tighter and tighter on them, they will be able to recognize the difference between love and fear. Reality and illusion. And in that recognition, they will choose love every time. And when they are ready, they will remember where they came from before they even put on this costume. This will be the beginning of their awakening into a much deeper level where life is no longer surfing the waves but is experienced in the deep and vast ocean where love is the body of water in which they can breathe freely. In this state of awareness, which can only be described as presence, there is a heightened level of consciousness. Your children will have the opportunity to experience true love and honor for self, and then for others. They will be capable of releasing emotional baggage from the past. And in time, as they continue to evolve spiritually, and begin to let go of blame and self-blame, they will remember where home is.

Home is not defined by bricks and mortar. I remember many years ago, I was forced by the courts to sell the home I raised my son in. My attorney made a comment that became invaluable to me throughout the years. He said something like this; "A house is just a pile of sticks. You can build a home anywhere." I really resonated with that on a deeper level. A house is not a home, and a home is not a family. Home is the heart and the essence of who you are. It is the embodiment of the soul. No memories, no divorce, no house, no move across town, no death, no loss and no relational break up can ever take that away from you. It is the formless home that is filled with infinite Divine love. It is the eternal home where we all come from and where we can all go to, at any moment that we feel the need to be reminded of that reality, as we navigate through this life on earth.

That said, we need to teach our children that which is formless. Not the vocabulary of the world in form that bleeds dependency of structure on them. Because when those structures break as they often do, from either sudden death, disaster or divorce, it makes the loss that much harder for them to cope with. Stability is found in peace, not in the structures of the world in form. Peace is that harmonious matrimony between one's self and one's inner child. One's self and God. Family is beautiful but goes much deeper than the family structure in which we are taught it is. Most children believe that a family consists of a mom, a dad, a sibling, maybe a pet or two, and a house. It is what they learn from society. They go to school at young ages and come home with crayoned drawings they created of a mommy, a daddy and a child holding hands in front of a house with a picket fence. It is what they are taught. Observing what your young child brings home from school that they personally create are wonderful ways of peeking through the window of their little hearts. My son went to a Christian School for five years. I remember one day my child came home with a project in the second grade. The children were asked to draw pictures that represented things that they feared in their life. They were to put these drawings, along with a real photograph of themselves as a baby into a small plastic strawberry container. On top of the container, they taped a scripture from the Bible that represented the weekly lesson they were learning about God's protection on us. My son was the only child that drew a picture like this: It was a picture of the house we lived in. In front of the house was a car at the curbside, with a man in the driver's seat of a car yelling things in bubbles that he drew coming out from his mouth through the window. Behind the car was a police car with flashing lights. Beyond that was a mom, and a baby holding onto his mother with crying tears that were drawn streaming from his eyes. This picture spoke volumes, and at the same time was quite disturbing. You don't have to be a brain surgeon to figure out that all of the minutiae and unconscious actions in post-divorce, instilled fear in the young child. The only thing we should instill in a child of a divorce situation is formless and infinite love, and how it is ever so possible to hold onto that love in the face of impermanence. This is done by your actions in each experience. Lead your children by loving example and give them the opportunity to experience acts of love and not fear. This will help them understand that which is formless, and how they can hold onto that formless love a midst the impermanence of life situations.

When we suffer loss, we experience degrees of pain within that particular experience. If it goes unaddressed, it gets added to the collection of past pain creating dimensions, if you will. Each dimension in its own space may differ from the next, but they all lead to the same end point. Pain. It has been said that time heals all wounds. When speaking of emotional wounds, I disagree. Time does not heal. Time allows us to suppress past pain. It also allows us to dwell in it by adding our stories to it and keeping the internal dialogue alive. In my view, we suffer in time rather than heal. When it comes to healing our emotional pain, it can only happen in the present moment. When we heal, we are at peace. Peace is felt in the stillness of the mind in the present moment. It is found in the calm space that permeates between thoughts. Conversely, time is a temporal dimension and there is no space in time. Time is a way of measuring physical change. We can almost expect a physical change in time. But when it comes to our heart and spirit, our natural essence which is formless, we must always come to a state of presence for healing. And in that presence is awareness, acceptance, and letting go. It is also a space for reprogramming if you will, where you can hear your new thoughts say, "I am okay." I see it as the new conscious ego arising.

What I would like all children and teens to take from these stories is that the essence of who you are is so much more than what you see through the eyes of the thinking mind. The truth of who you are stretch far beyond any vocabulary that you have been taught on this earth. You are part of the Oneness of the Universe that is heart driven by and through love. In truth, on the scale of the Universe, we are all connected. We are all of the same universal seed. So love yourself. Enjoy life as you walk through it. Stop trying so hard to prepare for life. You can never fully prepare. Life can only be now. Conversely, don't avoid life either. Never fear life. Love life. You do not have to protect life, and you do not have to solve life. Know that the situations in your life are of no absolute importance. The only importance at the end of the day will be how you loved and honored yourself, regardless of your life situations. And how you achieve things should always be through and with a loving heart. This is how we evolve as individuals and collectively. The heart is the doorway to wisdom. What you seek outside in the world, is already within you. You already have that which you are seeking. You just need to recognize it. You have the power to overcome, and the ability to claim love in your life. You are the embodiment of love and this love is your Divine and infinite free gift. So enjoy the journey, and remember that you can return home at any time, at any moment. Always.

The Butterfly

August 2012. It was a Sunday morning and I was resting in bed. My son was also in his bedroom resting. We had plans to get together with one of my best friends, whose son was also a good friend of my son's. We had spoken late Friday night, just a few days prior on the telephone and were looking forward to catching up that afternoon. My cell phone rang. It was a mutual friend of ours. She asked if I heard the news. She called to tell me that my girlfriend was struck by an automobile the day before on that Saturday morning while riding her bicycle. "Nooooooo...." I cried out as it echoed throughout the walls of my bedroom. My son came running across the cat walk of the house and entered my bedroom. I told him the news I had just learned. We sat there on my bed in shock. The days following, my son and I went to the memorial service and burial at the cemetery. The memorial service was heart-wrenching and yet, it was the most inspiring and loving event that I had ever experienced in someone's death. This would make sense as my dear friend was the embodiment of a loving spirit. I remember that her son stood with my son, outside of the room in which his mother's broken body was laid out. He refused to go in and view the dead body and said, "That is not my mom. She would want me to celebrate her life." How profound. He was absolutely right. I admired how convicted he was. Even in his mother's death, he knew that her spirit was alive and with that, I was convinced that our souls never die. I remember her daughter spoke and sang for all of us, and teenagers whose hems she touched, also spoke and danced in honor of her life here on earth. After a heartfelt ceremony, and the many tears which were difficult to hold back, my son and I went to the car to head to the burial with everyone else.

Fluttering and hovering at the window of my car was this beautiful monarch butterfly. It was so bright amidst the sudden rain that poured over us. Suddenly, I felt a sense of peace and calm. Previous to the presence of this monarch, I was what one might call a basket case. I stopped. I stared at the butterfly in silence. It stayed there sitting on my wind shield as it slowly and calmly kept fluttering its wings open and closed, and open and closed. I looked at my son and said, "I think that's Felicia." He said, "I think so too, mom." Off we went. Days went by and I planted beds of roses in my backyard alongside the in-ground pool. They flourished. I sat out there daily and spoke a lot to Felicia. Monarch butterflies would latch onto me so often while I was out there, for ten or so minutes at a time. I would call to my son to observe and we both smiled in amazement as we would say, "It must be Felicia." I sat out there daily until it was too cold to sit out there any longer, as the winter months approached. Was the monarch butterfly really her? It didn't really matter. What mattered was the observation of this monarch butterfly that awakened me on the day of Felicia's burial. For the first time, I really understood how we are all energy. Everything is energy and that energy is all part of the Divine Oneness that expresses love. I saw love in the monarch. I felt peace from the monarch. That butterfly and all of those that followed me thereafter and clung to me represented all of the things in this life that I had loved and lost and was coming back to me in a different form. When we lose a loved one, we gain love back in different forms.

When we have a great loss, there is also great possibility to awaken into a deeper level of consciousness, where the knowing of impermanence in this world no longer keeps you in suffering mode. That knowing can bring you a sense of peace beyond human understanding. The human intellect doesn't allow peace because it always wants answers as to how, and why, and resist what is. But if you can let go of the need for answers and just be, without resisting what is, you can awaken to a heightened level of consciousness and experience peace. You may still hurt for a while, but there will be a sense of peace that overcomes you in the acceptance of it. What I found in all of the loss I experienced from divorces to deaths, from houses to businesses, and so on, was that as we strive so valiantly for a happy future we are missing the moment we are in now. Happiness is here, and not over there. It is in the present moment.

When you experience loss, be careful that the good or bad memories you hold onto with such reverence do not rob you of the life you breathe today. Let me explain. We can honor a person who has gone on, and the joyful memories that are there. But we also need to let go of attachment to them, so that we can begin to notice and take in all of the surrounding love in this moment. It is always going to be moment by moment, and step by step. If you have bad memories with someone who has passed, be careful that you are not holding onto the added stories you have been storing in your mental warehouse. You will need to let these stories go so that you do not slip into a thought based mentality that speaks anger in your life. When we live in history or anticipation, we miss the mark. The target should always be to live in the moment. I find that to dwell in the past depresses, and to worry for the future stresses. If you want peace, don't get caught up in time. Throw away the mental event calendar. There is clock time, and there is event time. There is no greater deterrent to peace than time. So, be here in this moment. To live in the moment is to have found the crown jewels. It is to have found love. Try not to understand this on an intellectual level because it is just not possible. The intellect insists that everything in time and space comes with an explanation and is fill-able. It is just not fill-able. The truth is, nothing stretches before you or behind you. Anything other than the moment you are in now is an illusion. So be here in this moment, and try to grieve not. Trust that the Universe will bring you love in different forms.

The Affair

I lost my husband to violence, my franchise business to the recession, my home and possessions to divorce, my best friend to ego, and my mind to all of the madness. All within a short period of one year. I not only lost my mind but I lost the use of my heart. I was on the front lines of this battle that was trampling over me repeatedly. I judged my life during this time as a complete disaster. This was the second time in my life that everything in me, about me, and of me felt dead.

The straw that broke my back was the residential loss of my son. There is no other word to describe this pain. I just felt dead. I didn't care about possessions at all. All I cared about was losing life as I knew it with my son. My ego kept poking away at me, asking me if I was sure I made the right choice or should I have fought. Innately, I knew that I made the right choice because I chose to let go of the ego and end all of the suffering. What I discovered was that fighting the good fight is fighting for love. For Oneness with life itself. I decided to trust in the Divine and put peace back into all areas of my life. There was no peace in fighting, and I only saw fighting as a path toward disease and self-destruction. This was a pivotal moment for me. And so I knew I made the right choice, regardless of the intermittent echo of that inner voice in the head, which I decided would no longer run my life. At this point, I had already begun to awaken, so there were very conscious decisions that I made in my new present lifestyle. That was one of them.

During this time all I had left was my son's dog, our cat, and a parrot. I felt like Steve Martin in the film "The Jerk". My mindset was that I didn't need anything…maybe just this painting, and that goose down duvet. That's all I really need, I thought. I did have a few good friends though, which in this present day I call a few good men. One of them I will call Frankie, in which without his friendship, this book would not have been written. He was the one person I cried to when I had given up all hope in this journey called life. I felt that if my son was not living with me, I could not go on in life. I lost my purpose. I was feeling suicidal.

I wept like a baby at a bistro in public, which was so utterly embarrassing because I rarely let my insides out. I was throwing in the towel. My dear friend reminded me of my dreams that I had once shared with him. He encouraged me to hold onto them and go live my life, and basically start a new life. He told me of a story between him and his own son, to demonstrate how I made the right choice and that the circumstances would turn around for good, in due time.

I recall him advising me to move a distance away from the town that I raised my son. Personally, I felt that I needed to detach from all of the people there, positive and negative, and also the positive and negative memories. He agreed and also felt I should be far from something else that related to a secret I shared with him. This secret was embarrassing for me. But Frankie was a friend that I felt safety in telling. I believe that he felt I told him because he promised to put it in the vault. In truth, that wasn't why I told him. I told him because I felt he would not judge me. That was my biggest fear, and at the crux of my heart, I was in desperate need of non-judgment. It was debilitating enough to be judging myself, and so it was important for me to tell someone who would not judge me further.

The secret was that I fell into this affair with a married man for several months. This was at a time when I was feeling empty and had a big hole in my heart. I didn't feel that I was seeking love at the time because I had lost all hope in love. Having an affair with a married man was the furthest thing from what I would have expected from myself, none the less there we were, in this affair. We met while I was at work, and were attracted to each other both physically and intellectually. None of my family knew him, nor did I know his. We were not in the same circle of friends either. He knew I was single and divorced, and I learned he was married. We shared stories about our children, and that was the extent of family discussion. For whatever emotions we felt at the time, we pursued each other, and we were fully conscious of our decision to have this affair.

It was not a matter of meeting someone when you've consumed too much alcohol and consequently make a bad mistake. We were completely sober and planned out our time together during the work day. He set up a separate cell phone just for us to communicate together. We didn't physically see each other a lot, but we did talk a lot. So why do I tell you this secret? Clearly I am not proud of it, however, the affair was actually a life lesson that I needed to learn. The first thing I learned was awareness. Awareness of ego. I knew that I would never stay with this man or encourage the relationship to progress because of the obvious fact that he was married with children. I did not want to feel responsible for breaking up family ties. What I found most compelling was the idea of having someone like him. He was very caring, kind and tender with me. He was always very helpful when I needed him, and was a good friend to me. Similar to that day in the park with my baby on Mother's Day nearly twenty years ago, it was the act of love that I desired so much. This was because there was so much absence of it in my life. That was the recognition of the unconscious ego. What I learned from all of this was to let go of ego, and go to the heart to seek fulfillment. Not a person. In doing this, I chose to listen to it, and trust that the love of the Universe would put everything in its proper place for me, as long as I remained honest and true to self. And so, that is what I did.

After I moved away, I sent a quick text to him to say good bye, and the phone was no longer in service. I knew that was the Universe opening up opportunity for me, and that my new life experiences would be going in a positive direction. It was another pivotal moment for me. It was also another loss, but I didn't feel the need for any closure directly with this person because the Universe had given me exactly what I was asking for. What was I asking for? A return to love. Love of self. Fulfillment of self. The end of ego and the end of suffering.

I just wanted to be happy in my own skin. That is all I wanted. I wanted to feel joy amidst all of the pain I was feeling. The pain was still there, as were the sudden changes in my life situation, however, my heart was at peace because I understood that there was so much more for me in this life. I began to float in the perimeter around the pain and was able to live with it until I was ready to release it. This was my second lesson. Acceptance. Remember, as I mention earlier in this book, experiences are not your life. You are life. Life is so much deeper than that of what the unconscious ego tells you. And you have the power within to create the experiences that serve your highest good. When you can be in acceptance of a current situation, and take the action needed to close the experience and begin anew, you are able to create new moments that are fruitful and loving.

The third lesson I learned was non-judgment. I had to learn to let it go without judging the affair. It happened. It was the choice I made at the level of consciousness I was in at the time. This letting go was a big part of forgiving myself.

This letting go was also a big part of not judging my actions. Releasing it all allowed me to open new, positive, and beautiful experiences that covered me with grace and dignity. I became grounded and aligned with the Universe. I really began to understand the difference between that of form and that which is formless within myself. The formless is the essence of who you are beyond form which I discuss throughout this book. You can sense this as your spirit or soul, or infinite love. The form is what you identify yourself with in your physicality, your health, and your relationships with a partner, children, co-worker and so on. Imagine form as the transient you. When you can enter all life situations of form in this life through the eyes of the formless you, you have mastered life. This is because it is not the situations that matter, only how you navigate through them.

  This level of consciousness is amazing to me because it demonstrates how everything that used to seem important is not, and how everything that is important becomes evident. The only thing that matters after this body expires, is how we loved, how compassionate we were in all situations, and how gracefully we let go of things that no longer serve our highest good. I found that we really learn how to let go through loss.

I believe that we must experience loss if we are to grow.

"Trust hovers above logic in a space of uncertainty that just knows all is well."
~Lily Sanders

CHAPTER 12

The Liar on Your Shoulder

ONE OF THE SINGLE MOST DEBILITATING roadblocks on your journey to self-growth is fear. Fear is the little guy on your shoulder that tells you it is much safer to stay where you are, stagnant and on the road headed in the opposite direction as love. When we are in a state of fear, we are blocking out love and the possibilities of creating a loving life. It is so debilitating that we tend to lose our capability to love.

When you have lost the ability to love and feel love, it becomes all about survival and fear. This is not a healthy place to dwell. It is like living life through the reptilian brain, which is based on fear. The reptilian brain was the name a neuroscientist gave to the basal ganglia, structures derived from the floor of the forebrain during development. The term came from the idea that comparative neuroanatomists once believed that the forebrains of reptiles and birds were dominated by these structures. He proposed that this reptilian brain was responsible for typical species behaviors that involved aggression, dominance, territoriality, and ritual displays.

Having raised a green-cheeked conure for the twelve years since it is five months hatched, I somewhat understood this. I have learned much from observing my parrot, and understand the concept of how they are dominated by these structures. The reptilian brain keeps you in survival mode, where states of insecurity and anxiety fester. The problem arises when you stay stuck in survival mode as a state of being. You become locked in the reptilian brain and suddenly, everything seems like a threat to your survival, where there is always a problem to solve and danger to find. It reacts, and it reacts quite unconsciously. I have witnessed this with my parrot. I have also witnessed this in myself during my unconscious years and in other unconscious people. The characteristics of the reptilian brain range from territoriality, the hierarchical structure of power and control, ownership, jealousy, anger, hostility, anxiety, worry and fear, aggression, combativeness, and cold-bloodedness. Other characteristics range from obsessive compulsive disorder, hoarding, stealing and deception, to fight or flight behavior. The reptilian brain will overpower one's ability to have calm rational thought unless you come into conscious presence. So how can we re-wire here? By being present and tuned in. When we stop and observe the thinking mind and dis-identify with the thoughts and belief systems that have been embedded in there, we can disconnect from thought based fears, and begin to enter into an alert state of presence. Within this state of presence, you will have the ability to react differently. Observing my parrot was a great way to understand the concept of fight or flight behavior, and how much the reptilian brain is completely wrapped in fear. Looking back, there were times in my life when I could recognize where I personally made decisions based solely on my fears. This recognition became another life lesson where I can say with conviction, that I no longer allow fear to run my life. The love in my heart and the inte-grated connection I now have is powerful and divine. To live in this love is to blow the little liar off your shoulder every time. It allows innate to take over and intuition to steer the wheel. Your intuition will never let you down.

When I observe pain, I notice that fear is a close second. And when you believe the fear, the emotional suffering begins. When we are given a body threatening diagnosis from the doctor, we suddenly sense fear. We are afraid of the suggested treatments and its side effects, and even more afraid of it not working. We fear that we will never experience life as we knew it and that it may even come to an end. We promise ourselves and God that we will do anything to get the life back that we identified with. Some people say they would do anything for the chance of a do-over. They promise to stop smoking, start eating healthy, to give up this or that, and to be kind to others. The sickness, which we will call pain, has suddenly become a wake-up call. If pain is warning us to wake up or else...then why do we fear it? If there is a fire in your house while you are asleep, and a random fire fighter enters to wake and save you, do you fear the fire fighter can't save you, or do you embrace him?

One day the market crashes and all that you had goes with it. The few things you have left begins to wither away as well, and suddenly you have a mental and emotional meltdown. How can this be? The loss, which we will call pain, of what you had and all that you identified yourself with, has put you in a state of fear as a result of the pain. Your life spins deeper into chaos as you begin to push the people who love you the most out of your path, and you become angry at the world for not cooperating. Let us suppose that while you were living with all of the money and feeling secure, that you were actually sitting in the dark holding your breath the whole time. You appeared satisfied there but were actually too frightened to move. It seemed that you felt safe there, but deep down you feared that one day...this would happen. Perhaps you even unconsciously manifested it. The little liar on your shoulder said, "I told you this would happen!" Is it possible to see this fear as a window shade, stopping the light from getting in? Can you see how fear runs your life?

Remember, pain is not your enemy. Rather it is an opportunity for growth. If we fear our pain, we cannot address it. Be aware when you sense fear, but realize that fear is only an illusion that the thinking mind is telling you. Don't believe it. It does not really exist. Only in your mind. It is the little liar on your shoulder. When you say no to fear, you can begin to address the pain. This is where the important internal work begins. This is where you should do a self-

inquiry, and become aware of your pain. And in that awareness, there is an embrace…a holding on, where you know that
it has come to you for a reason. Come to know your pain as
something to love and embrace, not as something to be
feared. And in that embrace, you will find your truth. In a
way, pain can be a blessing because it can lead you to finding
your truth. It can be your passage into love and light. Remember that fear is the opposite of love. We cannot
transform if we are living in fear. The only way to transformation is through love.

Sometimes we will be on our way to an event or gathering, a family member's home, a city or even a country, and
suddenly we feel restless and uneasy. Perhaps you sense that
you are a little nervous, or you have an unsettled heart that
you cannot place your finger on. This is fear. This is the little liar on your shoulder. I find that this is another wonderful
opportunity to look inward and do your internal work. If fear
is the opposite of love, the first question you may ask yourself
is who have I not forgiven? You will be amazed to see what
unfolds within your own heart. It may be a friend, a family
member, a situation or even a country that you have not forgiven. This is where you should simply and unequivocally

forgive. Let it go. It has no influence over you now. If you do not release it, you will store it, and continue to suffer.

If love is absolute and fear is an illusion, why do we lose ourselves in illusion? If love is the infinite essence of who we are, why do we sometimes act out of fear and not love? A few times in this book I mention that we knew love all along, but have forgotten it because of all of the madness in the world around us and in our life situations. To the extent that we forget who we are, that piece of Divine Oneness in which we are all connected, we also forget love. And so we fall into this bottomless pit of pain. This pain brings us choices. We will either remember to love or act out unlovingly. When we act out unlovingly, it means we are still frightened. Chose love and not fear. The goal for us is always to return home. When I speak of home, I speak of love.

"If you do not guard your thoughts, that negative unloving narrative you let in can become the main source of the mental summary of yourself."

~Lily Sanders

CHAPTER 13

Gone With the Wind

NOT LONG AFTER LIFE SITUATIONS forced me to close my business, I was trying my best to keep this tremendous house together. Soon after that, there were a few record breaking snow storms and hurricanes that covered our town and surrounding areas. These were challenging times, in keeping up and surviving. Then there was Hurricane Irene that swept through our town causing devastation and damage to our homes. Two months later was the big Nor'easter of 2011. Then there was the record breaking blizzard of 2013 that overtook New York, literally by storm. It was devastating. I remember being outside after the hurricane and going up the road, searching and gathering pieces of the vinyl siding that once covered my home, and bringing them back to my property. There were gutters and leaders off and fascia hanging off the doorways. My son was at his friend's house experiencing the odd quiet that comes after a storm such as this. I remember the frigid weather freezing my body. I gathered all the pieces to the house, found the proper nails in the garage, and pulled out the tall ladder. I had no funds to hire anyone to help. The courts made me put my home on the market to be sold, and I was also responsible for its upkeep. I needed to put this house back together somehow by myself, and I was completely overwhelmed. I did not complain and did not ask for help. I remember being on the ladder and lining up the fascia around the front entry door. Nose frozen and numb, I began nailing a piece into place. For those years that I kept up the home, it wore me out physically and mentally. I was utterly exhausted and financially beaten. I recall one wintry night when I ran out of oil for the third time that winter, lying in the cold bedroom by myself and just crying all alone. I opened my bedroom door and told my dog to keep me warm till morning. That was the first invite he had in my room and onto my bed. Needless to say, for those readers with pets, it was like heaven on earth for the dog. I learned much from these times. I learned how to tile, plumb, excavate, landscape, and love. Each storm and every disaster were my teachers. Throughout these times I also dealt with people who forgot I was a human being. It is really okay because I remained honest in all that I did, and all that I endured molded me into the person I am now. It taught me much about the unconscious world we live in. I was always a hard worker, with perseverance and integrity. I am still all of that, except now everything in my life is aligned with the Universe. That is because I decided to love myself. No person, place, situation or circumstance could ever stand in the way of that love, ever again. To truly know this, was to find a treasure that had been hidden for so long. It took me years to remember where I left it. It is a freeing moment where you suddenly realize that all of the things you thought mattered, don't really matter at all. Those things eventually are all gone with the wind. The only thing that matters is the love that is left in your heart. Once you lose the ability to feel that, you have nothing. That is when you find yourself floating aimlessly in this abyss of pain. There are no riches or relationships in the world that can ever replace the infinite love in your heart. It is your free gift. When we can know love, with all of our senses, and then share it…we can move mountains when raising our children, and caring for others. If we can feel and express our inner love to our children through actions and experience, then we can begin to see a shift take place in collective awareness, and our children can break the mold for generational blessings.

Guard Your Thoughts

When parents act out in highly unconscious behavior in front of their children, they are teaching them suffering through experience, rather than love through experience. All children really want is to feel love and have peace. All adults really want is to feel is love and have peace. No one wants to feel fear and experience conflict. When a child experiences verbal attacks from their parent or witnesses this behavior from one parent to the other, or to a sibling, they store it in their mental warehouse. Negative verbiage creates an internal mental dialogue that says, "Oh. So this is what I am." For those reading this book that are aware of this internal conflict, don't buy into it. If you do not guard your thoughts, that negative unloving narrative you let in can become the main source of the mental summary of yourself. This is suffering. Let it go.

Lose it. Don't believe any of it. Know that you are amazing and perfect.

Teach your children to guard their thoughts, and if you are parenting, guard your mouth. Children will suppress what they have heard from their years growing up, and their mental interpretation of themselves from years of verbal abuse can become that of rejection, and fear. If your child is being told that they didn't do good yesterday, or that they will never become something worthy tomorrow, then you push them into a mental place that is far away from reality. All they hear in their thinking mind is what they weren't, what they are not, and what they will never be. As a result, children and adults alike can lose their ability to feel love for themselves, which is truly a death of the spirit. This is one of the greatest tragedies in life. Instead of experiencing love and peace in the present moment, they experience fear and conflict internally. This is where the suffering begins. It begins in the mind. Negative thoughts about ourselves or a situation are what creates suffering. All of the negative things we were told of ourselves, get stored in our mental warehouse. Let it go. Don't take ownership of it. Guard your thoughts. Know that there is nothing more precious than you in this moment. The things of the world are not precious. You are. They are to be honored and appreciated but know that they are transient. They will come and go. Time is not precious. You are. Use clock time to set goals and plan things, but know that you need not fully prepare for life because life can only be in the present moment. So in this moment, guard your thoughts like you are guarding your life. Fix your mind on your truth, and begin to plant new seeds that will grow you in a powerfully dynamic and positive direction.

Angels in the Hood

It was summer time of 2012 on Long Island, New York. It was around the time that I was just divorced and was forced by the courts to sell my home and split the proceeds of the sale with my ex-husband. There was much work to be done on the house and in order to get the best possible dollar for it, I needed to get it done. It was one of the hottest days recorded in 2012 and the heat wave was not letting up. The sun was powerful and scorching. It was a particularly challenging week. On the first day of the heatwave, I lead a few men that I hired and worked on the demolition of the old beat up wooden deck that spread fifteen hundred feet off the back of my house. Sweat emerged from my skin head to toe, as droplets poured down my nose uncontrollably just standing there. I recall my wet hands soaking through the garden gloves I was wearing. The gloves were necessary to grip the shovel I was using and to protect my hands from the splintered decking. I walked back and forth with yards of decking, plank by plank in my arms. I piled the demolished pieces beside the dumpster I rented. It was the largest dumpster to rent at the time, which was a twenty-yard dumpster. The three men I hired unmindfully kept throwing in pieces as they went along. The demolition was completed and yet, half of the decking was beside the dumpster and could not fit in. I called the company that I hired the dumpster from to make an inquiry. They maintained that the dumpster was definitely large enough, and could fit a small house if filled properly. I paid the workers, and they left. One of the workers I drove home because he had no transportation. I recall driving back to my house wondering how I was going to get everything into this dumpster by myself. My son was physically capable but seemed challenged in making himself available for house work. I imagine at that age it's more fun to hang with your friends. Since we know I was not good at force, and quite frankly I didn't want to add more stress to the situation, I didn't press upon it. I pulled into the driveway, went inside and put the air conditioner on. It was hot beyond words. I had two days left until the dumpster was to be picked up. I made myself an ice cold drink and went out back. I remember sitting in my filthy shorts, watching our dog play among all of the rubble. I started to cry. I felt alone and defeated. That's what my mind was telling me and I bought into it as I wept. The next morning I woke with a new mindset. I went out front to clean up the yard and get everything into that dumpster. I climbed atop the high dumpster and began to pull all of the large planks out of there. Then I jumped inside and layered the small ones strategically along the bottom floor of the dumpster. I climbed back out. I was dripping with sweat, and my hair that hung below my baseball cap down my back was stuck to my neck. My frail body was tired, I was emotionally drained and overheated from the sun. I climbed off and down the dumpster and stared at all of the large planks of decking. The amount of wood overwhelmed me, but I was determined to figure out the answer and do it. I kept staring at the sizes of the planks, the amount, and the twenty-five-yard dumpster. Suddenly, I knew what I had to do to make it all fit. I needed to cut these planks smaller so I could line them all up into the dumpster. Yes. But now what? Do I go rent a tool somewhere to start sawing these in half? All of a sudden, a sports utility vehicle slows down in front of my house and comes to a complete stop. A woman who I had never seen before, steps outside her vehicle and our conversation went something like this: "Hi. Wow…that's a big project!" "Yes. I need to cut these planks and pile them in." I replied. "My husband has a circular saw you can borrow if you want. We live just around the corner." I couldn't help but think she was an angel that pulled up, literally out of nowhere. I never saw this woman in my life. Since I never asked anyone for help, she was my angel. She was one of those people that appeared in my life for a short time, for the sole purpose of helping. It was a moment of realization that I had an absolute connection with the Universe. I needed help, and help appeared. I completed the tremendous project that most experts would say is a man's job and had everything fitting into the dumpster within two days. Till this day I am grateful for this neighbor who served as one of the angels the hood.

The next day, just after that demolition, I was out front again and onto the next project. Land excavating. I had thick rooted stumps from junipers that needed to be pulled and removed along with more brush that covered the berms. As I was pulling, my next door neighbor came out to work on her beautifully landscaped property. She came to greet me and offered to help me pull everything out. I insisted that it was back breaking and was hardly as enjoyable as planting or weeding. I will never forget her response. She told me that she loves doing stuff like that and convinced me that I needed her help. With that, I realized this was the second angel in the neighborhood that again, came out of nowhere. Till this day, I am forever grateful for her heart, her determination, and her muscles. She was another angel in the hood. It was at these times when I cried a lot from loneliness and overwhelm, that people like this kept appearing in my life. Again, there were those glimpses of light, and warmth that began to envelop me. Eventually, that light led me to finding who I am.

CHAPTER 14

Who Am I?

FINDING OUR PURPOSE seems to be trending these days. I suggest finding your 'who' before your 'what'. There are two curious questions many people have. Who am I, and does God exist? What if there was no who? What if we were made up of many constantly transitioning selves all connected with each other? What if the essence of our very souls were made up of a myriad of elements and not just one?

When I was a child growing up in a Christian home, science was considered to be a conflict with man-made religion and theological belief systems. What I noticed is that those who follow and teach doctrine seem to have fear in science, and its influences on religious followers. I imagine they feel science gives people the opportunity to question the existence of God. In my view that is ridiculous. I find that the more we learn about science, the more we learn about our Creator. Science explains things to us like time and space, different dimensions, energy fields, quantum physics and so on. Science is a systematic study of the structure and behavior of the physical and natural world by observation and also through experiment. If we can agree with the findings that science has made in the physical world, why do we struggle with adopting what science says about the natural world? We believe in gravity, although we cannot see it. We believe the earth revolves, although we cannot feel it. We believe it because science tells us this. However, when science talks about intelligent design, why do religious people run the other way? Is it fear of the unknown, a direct conflict of their belief systems, or both? I explored this, having been on both sides of the fence personally. I concluded that most people who admit to believing in God, see God as an energy in the sky, if you will, that is going to judge you. Then there are the people who are offended by that concept, so much so that they deny there even is a God. These are typically the people known as atheists, who deny any mystical label like Divine, Creator, or God. If we looked at it scientifically, where science explains how the natural world is all connected in one unified energy field, then it does give us a sense of Oneness. Whether you believe it or not doesn't exclude your connection to Oneness, however, it is our free will that separates us from it. We are all a piece of this spiritual core. It is ours, and yet it is who we are. You may even view this core as the essence of all of us. That is who you are. The essence of our souls is not singular. We see singular when we look at each other and in the mirror. But the person you saw in the mirror when you were five years of age, is clearly not the same person you see today, is it? Of course not, because this human body is transient and in time, will change. Remember, time is a way we measure physical change. Our thoughts and emotions and dreams change as well. The essence of who you were as a baby, is not the essence of who you are now. The dreams I had as a child are not the dreams I have now. Some of them may be, and yet others are new and different. Can you see how the essence of your soul is multiple? This concept all made sense to me when I began to search for meaning in life. I read many books on respected spiritual teachings, philosophers, scientists, and inventors ranging from The Holy Bible to Buddha to Nikola Tesla. In my searching, I was brought to first seeking within. That discovery began to multiply as it included everyone and everything in creation. It is much more than just you and me. We are all part of a whole. We are all intrinsically connected and have the heart, intelligence and power to love, heal and serve. My journey brought me back home. Again, when I speak of home I speak of love. As an important piece of the Divine Oneness, we are given free will. You can allow the spirit in you to feel love, to be kind, and to heal yourself and others. That said, it is safe to suggest that to love, to express love, and to use the powerful energy field in which we are universally connected to heal, is our innate purpose.

First, we need to experience an awakening. A spiritual rebirth so to speak. Some people are not comfortable with the word 'spiritual'. If you are one of those people, perhaps I can suggest not getting so caught up in the language. If it is not of the physical body, it is spiritual. Don't complicate it. Keep it simple. Your awakening or enlightenment is an aha moment in life where the dimmer switch is turned way up. Then there is that wonderful transition where you will mature in your spiritual growth. Suddenly, all of the things you sensed and knew all along and were drawn to, begin to pop up, all in its appropriate timing. This is an example of Divine timing in one's life. Being aligned with oneself and the Universe can help you understand that there are cycles in life, and they need to be honored. Stop blocking the creation of what you are asking for and instead, be the creator of your own reality. Once you understand that you are one brush of this universal canvas, you can create anything. If you find that you are in the froth of adversity, ride the energy of it instead of fighting it. This can be a powerful time of self-growth. Stay present in all that you are transitioning through. Be cognizant of all that you see and hear, because that massive energy that is constantly being created is what will change your life.

So how can you begin to change your own life, and then go on to help others? Who are you at this moment, beyond the human costume you wear? Who are you in this moment without the labels? Who are you in this transient moment, regardless of the situation surrounding you? If you could undress, and simply be in that space of conscious awareness without self-judging, without comparing yourself to others, and without resistance to what is, it would come down to two choices. You will either decide to love yourself or destroy yourself. Which will you choose?

I recall watching an interview many years ago with comedian actress Lucille Ball. She was asked the differences between her former husband, Desi Arnez who was deceased at the time of the interview, and her current husband who was sitting beside her. She said, "He's not a loser. I married a loser before." She didn't say it with a judging spirit. She went on to explain that her first husband could win everything, at very high stakes, work very hard and was brilliant, but he had to lose. What a profound statement. I understood exactly what she meant. Some people choose love, while others choose to lose love. It is that simple and also that tragic.

The Wounded Puppy

It was a crisp morning, and the array of yellows, reds, and oranges blanketed the ground. The newborn puppy pushed its way out through her mother's canal last. The absence of sight and sound kept her dependent upon mom's nursing and loving care. Four pups whimpered and cried, slept and cuddled, as they lay tucked away in their den. Weeks passed, and the pup could see the light of day and hear the birds calling. Winters came and went, as did summers. One day the pup's father went astray during a crashing bang in the air and bolting light in the clouds. Soon after the storm, her mother went gallivanting as she explored unknown territories that spread wide behind the face of fear. That was when the pup began to befriend other puppies in the area. It wasn't long before she had become attached to a handsome pup nearby. They played and loved for years. One day, she found him frolicking about with another puppy. She felt betrayed and left the neighborhood. Running as fast as she could through the wooded terrain, the pup decided to enjoy her new surroundings and explore everything that made her little tail wag. She was content for some time until suddenly she realized she was lost in the forest and far away from that den she remembered many seasons ago. She journeyed through the forest with a few young dogs, all of whom eventually parted, due to storms, challenges in the terrain, and even sudden death. The wounded puppy continued to live in terror, inside the grown dog as she periodically surfaced as the dog's emotion and pain. That wounded puppy was me.

The puppy is anyone's inner child. It is a metaphor for the inner child of a human being, and its den is a metaphor for home. And when I speak of home, I speak of love. Infinite and unequivocal love resides within. This is your innocence. This is your inner child. Perhaps it has been obscured through the madness of life situations and unconscious living. Use this madness as your stepping stones that return you back to love. When you connect to your inner child you may feel the energetic debris. Once that awareness is there, you can begin to release the energetic patterns that were created by those parts of your inner child that no longer serve you. It is said that we are constantly creating our experiences, our illnesses, and diseases. If this is so, then we also have the power of dis-creation. We all have the power to remove karma and give the Universe immediate command to unravel these karmic progressions. This power comes from love. Love is the healing antidote for your inner child. Embrace your inner child with love, then release all of the energetic debris that needs releasing to clean your house. You are responsible to clean your own house. No one else. Restore your energy field. Everything else will fall into place as perfect pieces to a magnetic puzzle. These energetic pieces are designed to work for you and with you. Inside of you and outside of you. They are quantum. Try not to understand it as human intellect or logic. Quantum love cannot be challenged. It *is*.

"Love brings answers and wisdom that stretch far beyond human logic."

~Lily Sanders

CHAPTER 15

Love Is

TO FIND SOMETHING, we must first determine what exactly it is that we are seeking. It took me decades to find love because I had no clear picture or understanding of what it was. I only knew what was taught about love in this world, and none of it seemed deep enough to me. In my view, what I found was that most of what the world says and teaches about love causes confusion, frustration, and depression. When I discovered the truth about love, I had no more questions about life. It was a feeling and a knowing of completion. So, what is love? How does it look, feel, smell and taste? What might it sound like? Where would it hide?

Love is the essence of all consciousness. Love is the stimulus for everything in life. It is the yeast that develops and gives rise to our daily bread. *"Give us our daily bread...*" It brings answers and wisdom that stretch far beyond human logic. When we give up the constant struggle and conflict going on in the mind, love enters in. Because our very essence at its core is love. When we came into this world we were taught survival.

Everything we do, eat, see and breathe is all about our need to survive on this planet in this human costume. The focus is on how to get this, and where to get that. The world teaches children to stress about the grades they need to accomplish, and the college they need to get into. Then we stress about how and who is going to pay for it. We long for that special wedding that is supposed to resolve our search for endless love, and then we grieve after loss and fight during divorce. It is all a continuous race we are on, up one hill and down the next, and yet the finish line changes all the time. It never ends. It is as if there is no finish line. The only glimpses of love you experience in this race are transient cups of water that you get from the side lines. The water replenishes you for the moment, and then you continue the race until you reach the next check point. The result is a cluttered mind of unrest and disillusion. This constant static in the mind that you have become accustomed to is the very thing that shields you from love. If you can surrender to everything you thought was supposed to happen and everything you think is going to work, love will enter.

Stop sitting in the dark trying to figure out your life problems. Don't overthink how to do something that you do not know. 'You don't know what you don't know' is a statement I have heard many times in the past, and up until recently I finally understood it. Once we can disengage with the logic of our minds and drop the fear barriers, the solutions to life problems and answers that we seek not only begin to surface, but become crystal clear. Stop overthinking the how do I's, and simply allow yourself to not know what you don't know. Just allow it to happen. *"Be still and know"*. Listen to that intuitive voice. It has been said that intuition is the voice of God. When you go inward, you can hear it. There is great multi-dimensional wisdom in that stillness and listening. That knowing and that voice do not come from logic. It is the nonlinear wisdom that comes from a deeper force that is far greater than the human intellect. There is a sense of trust in the giver of this wisdom, even though you cannot see it. But you need to stop, look, and listen in order to hear it. Shut off the mental noise in the mind that obscures love from entering.

Because truly, fear comes from the unconscious mind, not the heart. The heart houses love. Embrace it. Hear it. Share it. It is why we are here.

Love has no agenda and needs no introduction. It requires no initiation fee and need not be activated. Love *is*. It is the greatest energy on the planet. Love is the key ingredient of human consciousness. After all, God is Love. And if we are created in God's image then it would be safe to suggest that our very essence is love. Love is the catalyst to everything in life. If we can fuse our hearts with the love of God, we understand true agape love. Love is not prejudiced and is for all of humanity waiting to be found under every stone unturned. Don't let life situations keep you from love. If you find yourself amongst the rubble, keep turning those stones. There you will find love. Embrace it, because this agape love is an unconditional and universal love that transcends, no matter what your life situation is. It is the one thing you can count on. Trust it. Let the walls down and let the light in. The light will get brighter and shine on all of mother earth as you exercise your muscle of intuition. Trust in it. Let the light triumph over the darkness in your life and in others. Be the light. The light has always been with you. Let it shine. Let it shine on your city, your country, and on all of mother earth. *"You are the light of the world. A city on a hill cannot be hidden." Matthew 5:14*

We experience love in various ways. It seems that we are always on this quest for love. We are taught that love is found in a relationship between two people or with things. Love can be experienced within a friendship, or an intimate relationship, or between a dog and its human companion for instance. But this is not where absolute love is found. Love is found in pure consciousness. Love needs no partner to be felt. It only requires your recognition and attention. When we recognize love as the infinite energy that fuels us, we can begin to love *self*. Once we experience self-love, which is essential for inner peace, we can connect that with Divine Love. When you accept and love yourself just as you are, a true partnership emerges between you, your heart, and spirit. There is a connectedness that is experienced that can only be described as Oneness. And in that Oneness, you can begin to experience love in all things. You can see love in a beautiful landscape. You can feel love for a cat. You can smell love in a fragrant flower. You can touch love when you hold your child's hand. You can taste love when the salt from the ocean's breeze touches your lips. You can hear love in the happy birds that are chirping outside your window in the morning. Love is as it is. Pure consciousness. It is that conscious state where all senses can feel, and no conclusions arise. It is the gift that rests in your heart and holds boundless grace, infinite wisdom, and natural perfection. *"Be perfect, therefore, as your Father in heaven is perfect." Matthew 5:48*

Once you have found this true love of self, it connects you with Oneness. This is where we can connect pure consciousness with Love. Everything else we experience as love is transient. Love of a human relationship, love of a pet, love of a place or object...they all come and go. They are fleeting. We can certainly enjoy these love experiences and it is wonderful. But know that these external experiences are transient. But the love of God is everlasting. Love and Oneness never ends. This is our happily ever after. This is our once upon a time in the fable of all fables, that goes on and on, as the vibration of quantum energy called Love. This is your truth. Never let go of your heart in any situation in life. Let your heart be your safety net. Let it be that hand that

squeezes you every time you forget that you are pure consciousness.

When it comes to the topic of God and the love of
God, I find there is much confusion, frustration, questions,
and avoidance. Some refuse to talk about it, others get in
heated discussions over it, while still others run in the opposite direction from it. It seems to me that various doctrinal
teachings and interpretations have confused many, and perhaps have chased many away from God rather than closer. In
truth, what I learned is that Divine Love is our free gift and is
not something up in the sky that needs to be earned. A Creator has not put us in existence to be judged, but rather to be
loved. I suggest that if you have been judging yourself and
feeling you are not worthy, then stop. You are worthy and
you are deserving of love. It begins with you loving yourself
and choosing to connect with Oneness. So come to your quiet
place and let go of all judgment and fear. Claim love for
yourself. This is your birthright. Your purpose is to come to
know the loving 'I am' that you are. This is your truth. Your
gift. The Light.

And in that space of pure consciousness and love, you
can connect with the brain. I have mentioned this in earlier

chapters. Connecting the heart, intuition and the brain is where alchemy happens. This is the grander picture if you will, of who we are. This trilogy within us as human beings hold life altering power. Use it.

In 1991, there was groundbreaking research in the field of neuro-cardiology. Sensory neurons were discovered in the heart. Data showed that these brain-like neurons can process information and make decisions independent of the cranial brain. This incredible discovery established that the heart is a sensory organ and a sophisticated information encoding and processing center sufficiently qualifying as a 'heart-brain'. The concept of this functional 'heart brain' was first introduced by researcher neuro-cardiologist Dr. J. Andrew Armour. It is inspiring to see how science is beginning to parallel with ancient spiritual teachings. Today, science views the heart as a complex, self-controlled and organized system that maintains a continuous dialogue between the brain and the rest of the body. Astounding! This suggests that the heart is a mindful muscle if you will, and perhaps its sole purpose is not just to pump blood. If we can learn to connect the heart, intuition and the brain, imagine how much healing and love we could accomplish as a global family on this earth? We could move through a mindful heart, and take wise and intuitive actions to move mountains.

Some experts say that we have sufficient energy resources and food, the best technology, and the knowledge to end a lot of suffering on this planet. If this is so, then truly we are capable to do this as a global family if individually, we could connect all three. What's more, we can begin to live long and healthy lives as individuals. Science is now catching up to the spiritual wisdom that has been here all along. This is a wonderful time of change and transmutation on this earth, where the potential is there for the arising of global healing and shared support. In my view, it takes shared compassion to a whole new level. That said, the capabilities before us when connecting the heart, intuition, and the brain can feed the hungry, provide shelter and electricity, maintain overall well-being, and heal ourselves from sickness, imbalances, and disease. We are able. We can do this as a global family as we make strides toward a collective conscious shift. It starts with one. The righteous domino has already been put into place for the rest of us to align with. So let's do this! Let us begin to erase our stories of loss and separation and rewrite a new powerful story of connection and Oneness. Why in the world would we not want to move from a life of conflict and struggle to a life filled with synergy and calm? And isn't it about time that we let go of all of the fear and resistance in external life situations, and come into the love and acceptance of truth? If we could do this, we could start moving those internal mountains that no longer serve our highest good. After all, the shift must first begin internally. And as the war with your unconscious thinking mind dissolves, natural cooperation and healing throughout the body can take place.

It has been said that our thoughts can make us sick. If this is true, then can't our thoughts also make us well? If our thoughts are that powerful to do harm then imagine how powerful they are to do good? Our mindset and its collaboration with the 'heart brain' has the potential to change lives. This is a time of ascension. If we are going to swim to a deeper level of collective consciousness, we need to connect and not separate. Fear separates. Love joins. Fear disconnects. Love connects. Fear says it wants to protect you and keep you safe. But to know love is to be safe. After all, when love is present what is there to fear? Nothing. Let love be your 'go-to' source for energy. There is no greater source of energy in the Universe and beyond than that of Love. Remember I am not suggesting that fear doesn't show up because it does. In fact, it never misses an opportunity to interrupt peace, and always comes knocking. But be aware when fear is talking, and don't believe a word it utters. This is not denial. It is taking control of your own thoughts and connecting to your loving truth. This loving truth is the light.

With practice, that light gets brighter and brighter, and things become more and more clear. The light will naturally begin to shine on others. When we turn on a lamp light, we don't hide it under a blanket, do we? We allow it to light our path and everyone in it. Don't worry about others being bothered by the brightness. If it's too bright for someone who is not ready to leave the darkness, they will put up their own barriers to protect themselves from that light. These are the walls that people put up because they are still living in fear. Let it be as it is. Don't judge it. Your only purpose here is to turn the light on. We are not here to force light on others, however, we have no reason to hide it, and yet every reason to share it. Conversely, when the light shines on someone who has been in darkness their whole life, the potential is there for them to encounter an openness and a doorway that one might describe as an awakening. An awakening from light into darkness. From unconscious to conscious. It holds the possibilities to wake, stimulate and energize. Light has an infectious reaction on others. People are generally happier when the sun is shining. Their energy is boosted and their moods become upbeat. When humans feel the warmth from the sun there seems to be a connectedness and unexplained energy that feels good and natural. The same holds true with the light from within. So be the light. Remember, it costs nothing to love and costs everything not to. Live in love.

Acceptance

Be in acceptance of what is and allow your soul to guide you back to the only thing that matters. Love. This may cause you to feel out of control with a current situation or person in your life. Is it possible for you to observe a current situation and ask yourself, "What is it I am trying to control and why?" Realize that the Universe has given you this incredible opportunity to release the need to control. There are rhythms and rhymes to everything in life. Your marriage was not a mistake, and your decisions were not accidents. Your career choice was not a mistake, and how you arrived at it was no accident. In truth, every life situation you experience are moments of Divine design. Maybe there is a situation or person that you do not see eye to eye with. For this moment, can you observe the emotional build up that your feelings are creating because of non-acceptance? And can you put a pure conscious sphere around it? Instead of acting on the emotions, stop, be still, and listen to what your mindful heart is telling you. You may discover compassion for a person or situation, or perhaps instinct will tell you to respond with silence and walk away in effortless grace and dignity. That is innate. Take these moments and see them as enormous gifts in practicing grace. Realize that being in acceptance of a situation or person does not mean you are condoning that behavior or that you support it. It means you have begun to integrate, and see things at a much deeper level. You are ready to evolve and serve your highest good.

Once you accept your truth, you can transcend any circumstance, move beyond any experience, and begin to create new experiences that serve your highest good. In this new found light, you will understand and experience the daily bread of life. 'Our daily bread' which most recognize as a

Biblical term, was not only a request for physical provision, but for practical, emotional, relational, and spiritual needs. Many feel God sustains us physically and meets less tangible needs in this world of form. More than that, however, God fulfills our spiritual needs. Whether you choose to understand the bread of life concept in a Biblical or non-Biblical sense makes no difference. The point here is that the bread of life represents fulfilling our spiritual hunger. That which is formless. When we are filled with spiritual nutrients, the body and mind join harmoniously for overall well-being. Body, mind, and spirit are meant to work together. We live moment by moment, and one step at a time. Because of this, we need to spiritually connect in all areas of life.

If there is anyone who feels they do not need spiritual fulfillment, they are missing the mark on how to attain true agape love, which always comes from Source. We all need to go somewhere within, to connect to that Source. Some refer to Source as God, Universe, Creator, or energy. It is not doctrine. It is not religion, and it is not idolatry. It simply *is*. Not believing in what is, and the affinity of the Universe does stop it from being. Conversely, being open to what *is* will bring you home. The old saying *'home is where the heart is'* should actually be considered as a sutra. Hallmark may not have realized just how profound that statement truly is.

"You were given the Divine gift of love within, which far exceeds any temporary pleasures that the external world can bring."
~*Lily Sanders*

CHAPTER 16

How Can I Forgive?

MUCH OF OUR PAIN and internal struggles come from non-forgiveness. Not just toward others, but for oneself. A huge discovery for me was that I stored a lot of self-blame and self-judgment for all of the disasters in my life situations. I didn't know why and it didn't really matter. The only thing that mattered was that I came to a point of realization that there was something inside that needed letting go of. There was this black ball of conflict clogging my right to feel love and be happy. I just didn't love myself and didn't feel worthy of love. Only at the time, I didn't know it. Outwardly I appeared one way and inwardly another. When I dug deep and saw that my internal dialogue was so negative about myself, I became acutely aware of all of the self-blame and self-judgments that I had been storing up. This was largely because of my inability to negate what unconscious people in my life path were feeding my brain. The good news is that once we recognize that there is a blockage then we can remove it. But we need to go to the core. What is fueling this struggle and who is in charge of it all? We already learned in previous chapters that we need to know our 'who' before the 'what'. Once we know that, we can work on the how. What is fueling the struggle is absence. Absence of love. That is self-love. The one in charge of it all is your thinking mind. The mind tells you to fear, to hold grudges, to draw conclusions, to compare, to ignore and suppress, and to blame. In many cases, it will convince you to do this with yourself. There lie the blockages that are robbing your peace.

You can take your power back and turn it all around to exactly where you are destined to be. In self-love, and aligned with the Universe. When we have something inside that we need to let go of, like non-forgiveness and self-blame, it is going to come down to one thing. One question. The same question that seems to be at the top of the human mind's bucket list. Who am I? It is also one of the most powerful spiritual questions when we go to our heart in meditation.

This one answer will bring you home. Because who you are is love.

What I found is that it is helpful to pose a series of questions of oneself when it comes to seeking the answer to this universal question. I will discuss how to do this later in the chapter, but first, let's learn 'the who'. In chapter fourteen I discussed this and suggested that we are not singular, but multiple expressions of Oneness. Remember that we are transient beings throughout life. Because of this, what we remember as a baby, and from childhood, or even yesterday is not so important. The only thing that matters is that you remember who you really are. Finding that out will depend on what choices you make in your daily, moment by moment life situations. This is why being conscious is so key. So much stuff is thrown at us from birth until now, that it's no wonder why we have a junkyard full of meaningless stress in our busy minds. Beyond all of the minutiae, it will boil down to one ultimate choice. That is the choice to love. This is the only thing we need to remember. Just be who you are. Trust who you are. Trust Love.

Blaming is one way to be certain you stay trapped in your problems. You blame ego, you blame others, and you blame yourself. But who is self? Remember, you are not your mother, and you are not your father. You are not the labels you put on yourself or that others have put on you. So if you are not any of these things, then who are you really? Perhaps this one question brings up many others, and your mind might ask, *"Am I the good person that I was taught to be? Am I the grown up child that my mother or father wants me to be? Am I the parent that my children call upon me to be? Am I the brother or sister that my sibling expects I be? Am I the partner that my lover desires I be? Am I the successful person that I demand myself to be?"* These thoughts swim through your mind while pondering the one question. And doesn't it all seem like too much to answer? It is like a tidal wave trapped in the mind that keeps pulling you under and tumbling you around. Isn't it about time you went deeper? What if you were to stand up to the questioner in your mind? Ask the questioner, "Good for who and why? What is it I am supposed to do? How is it I am expected to be? Success according to what? And why does it depend on how well I perform on this stage that has been set, in order to be and feel worthy?" This war that goes on in the mind is the very thing that keeps us from self and Oneness. It keeps us stuck in a continuum of problems. As long as you stay wrapped in the illusion of the mind and everything it says you should do, be and act, then you will remain in darkness. This darkness keeps you from knowing who you truly are. It covers the light. Focus for a moment on the one who stands up to these questions in the mind. Who is the one who just inquired? Your innocence. Your inner child. The light. When I first heard about the inner child decades ago, I didn't get it. Not really. But what I did hold onto was the concept of this infinite soulful being that represented far more than the human shell I was born into. In and out of the years I casually readdressed the idea of the existence of the inner child. About ten years ago, that idea became invaluable to me during my process of forgiving others as well. When someone has hurt you and you're challenged with the understanding of it, it can be helpful to envision that person as a little innocent child or baby. There is a sense of knowing that enters the heart that tells you that we are all born with this innocence and have lost it in the madness of our individual life circumstances. Realizing this, helped me to forgive others. The real work for me, however, occurred within and was to be the beginning of my pursuit in finding my inner child and forgiving myself.

What I found is that a shift needs to take place within, where we can embrace our inner child and forgive oneself for denying it all of these years. Because in truth, if we are in self-denial, then we are not acting out in the perfect Love that we truly are. The awareness of and the concept of approaching and embracing my inner child sounded so weird to me at first. As you recall, this inner child concept was introduced to me back in the late 1980's. But it wasn't until recent years that I revisited this, and decided to give it a whirl. When I began to love, speak with, listen to, and unite with my inner child, there was a transformation that took place. That love connection between you and your inner child is also your connection to Oneness. Again, what is the inner child? The inner child is your innocence that you were born with. It has always been there, but you have forgotten it, as the disguises you wear and the human logic you have been taught, have interrupted your ability to embrace it. If you were to love, hear and listen to your inner child, what might he or she be trying to say to you? *"I am your innocence and I love you. I want you to love me because to love me is to love yourself. And to love yourself is to love God. You are worthy. You are perfect love just as you are."* So who are you? You are the light that has come into the world to transform darkness, and in the end, you will come to remember the only thing that matters. Love. I put the previous examples of questions between the mind and the inner child in quotations, so you can reflect on these questions and statements when you do your inner work. This became the time when I knew I was a light worker. Only, I had never heard of the term before and had no intellectual knowledge of it. It was purely an inner knowing that spoke from spirit.

Forgiving is the first step for healing in the body, mind, and spirit. Science has made new discoveries establishing that we have the natural ability to heal ourselves. Spiritual teachers have been professing this for centuries. We are hardwired to tap into healing on a molecular level as intuition speaks to our cellular structure. If we connect that with the love of self and our Creator (which is essentially Oneness), imagine how much more we can heal on a deeper level? Since we are all made up of energy and are all connected to this vast universal energy field, why couldn't we pull what we need from it? We can. Love is the most powerful energy force on the planet, and it is free. I believe that when we can clearly see a healthy, happy self and can vibrate with the frequency of having this as our birthright than we can heal. I trust that one day, with the altering of vibrational frequency in one's body to promote healing, we will continue to raise the vibration of energy on the planet, and recognize all holistic forms of balancing and healing, as a viable path to maintaining total well-being.

CHAPTER 17

How Can I Contribute?

WE CONTRIBUTE BY SERVING others, even in the work place. We do not need money to contribute. We need to contribute love. That will begin with self-love and then love and compassion toward others. It is the simple things, the subtle acts of love and kindness that can change the vibrational energy of love on this planet. In my conscious and triumphant years, I write, research, and interview different people around the globe. This is my current contribution. I recently went to El Salvador to do research for my next book and to interview people who had a sudden loss in their lives. My intent was to meet them, hear their story, and help them transmute their pain into peace. A dear cousin of mine arranged the interviews and did simultaneous translations where needed. I met with five women who I did not know, that shared their stories as I asked them questions. Each of them are reminders to me of my experience with shared humanity. Shared compassion. It was a perfect illustration of the mutuality in the experience of pain, no matter what the story is. The essence of what was left when I removed their stories was the undeniable pain. This was proof that pain is not our individual burden. I introduced the concept to them of removing the story and being open to feeling what was left. There was intense emotional pain that surfaced for some of them, and I could feel the heat of their suffering that laced their words and lingered in their moments of silence. When I returned back the states, I interviewed another young woman. Each of the life situations they experienced are completely different.

I honor each of them for their openness and allowing me to work with them and be a light to torch upon their own inner light. Their honesty and transparency have grown me in this quest to knowing Oneness and has poured compassion in my heart for them, and the world collectively. As I mentioned in earlier chapters, when we come to experience compassion on a universal level, our own experience of pain seems to lessen because there will always be someone else that is better or worse off than ourselves, and that our issue and circumstance just is. Saying yes to what is, will pave your way into presence. There is promise that presence gives in the surrendering of your own unhappy story. I ask that you be aware of how the Universal Law of Relativity demonstrates a connectedness between compassion and pain. What I found is that there is a tie back to compassion when we experience pain, and when we see other people's pain. For me, to go somewhere foreign and request of someone I do not know to share their story and their painful experience was part of my contribution to humanity that ultimately filled my own heart with more love and compassion than I ever anticipated. Many of these beautiful souls that I met had come from different walks of life, raised in different cultures, spoke different languages, and live in different economic and societal environments. In these next pages, I will briefly share some of their experiences. I knew that their life situations would be different than my own, however, it became crystal clear to me that pain is something we share universally, and to be able to feel another's pain, particularly that of a stranger is to have defined true compassion. Once you realize that we all experience pain at one level or another, it will open your heart to compassion for all of humanity.

As I share some of these stories, you will notice that although the circumstances in one person's life situation differ from the next, you can see there are distinct parallels between them, when considering matters of the heart. Regardless of gender, age, race, cultural and societal differences, we all have the ability to feel and exercise collective compassion. What I found was that although these differences make up a large part of our human experience, all of us share one common denominator. The internal burning desire to feel connected to self. To experience self- love, and to find our higher self or deeper power if you will, in connection with Oneness. Finding and knowing that 'I am' in every life situation in our human experience may be the very purpose for our existence. It may very well be our true inner purpose. It is the critical part of the human experience that takes us to a much deeper level reminding us in every moment of the 'I am' in every life circumstance that arises. And that 'I am' is changing all of the time because our life circumstances change all of the time.

When looking at the Universal Law of Relativity, we know that our circumstance at the moment simply is. The key is to say yes to it. Say yes to what is. Saying yes to this moment regardless of what appears to be happening, is saying yes to your truth. This is being. This is connecting with your loving truth. That loving truth is infinitely connected to the light. The Universe. God. However, you come to the light does not matter. There is no right or wrong way to it, really. Because truly, if being in a dark place brought you to your truth, then we can say that even the darkness can guide you to the light. The following stories show how their dark places have provided them a potential passage way into the light.

As if I do not Matter

I sat with four adult women and a small child in a Hotel lobby in El Salvador. I was a midst three generations. The mother, her three adult daughters, and her granddaughter. Teresa was the mother. Her husband was struck by a sugar cane truck and killed, never to return home to his wife, adult daughters, and his grandchild. It was a sudden loss that they were all trying to cope with for the past year. After interviewing these women, I sensed an enormous amount of suffering from the Teresa. She told me that she was going to a support group and seeing a psychotherapist for the past year. I asked her if she was learning to accept her pain. She said no, but she was learning to minimize the pain. I asked all of the women the same question. "When you think of the loss in this moment, how does it make you feel?" I told them that they would probably all have different answers, as we all experience loss differently. They did. Teresa's response was tremendous. She shared that when she thinks of her husband's passing, she thinks of her mother's death. When she thinks of her mother's death, she remembers how she had to become the mother and care giver for all of the three siblings and another four-year-old child in the household. She added that it forced her to grow up fast and it was very hard for her. I then asked her again, "How does it make you feel? She responded, "I feel as if I do not matter." She looked down. My eyes welled up, I embraced her, and she wept. Her daughters remained strong but held tears in their eyes. Until that moment, they didn't realize that mom had no self-worth and felt she was somehow unworthy of happiness and love, because of the courses of events in her life that she was still identifying with. It seemed that this was a new realization for Teresa as well. There was a sense of peace and openness around the table in which we sat. Not only did I remind Teresa that she was completely worthy of love and happiness, but I also validated the pain she was storing, and we were able to transform that suffering into peace. She was in acceptance of what was, and I went on to coach them as a family and how they can experience love and happiness in the new things of this present moment. It wasn't before long that laughter covered us around the table in which we sat. I am touched by the generosity of Teresa's heart and trust she has come more and more into presence, as she embraces self-worth and peace into her life.

She was a Miracle

I sat in the living room of a small house in El Salvador. When I began to interview this lovely woman, her eyes lit up as her first words uttered, "She was a miracle." The story was that her doctor looked at her during the birth of her daughter Francesca, and said that the baby was dead. The doctor told her there was no heartbeat, and to accept her death. "I did not accept and a few minutes later the heart beat started. It was a miracle!" she said. She went on to tell me that her daughter grew up healthy, and people spoke of her as the sunshine. She showed me photographs of her daughter and told me that there was a terrible accident by the beach. A young girl came to her home in the middle of the night to tell her there was an automobile crash and she was killed. She told me that she was in denial, just as she was the day her daughter was born. Only this time, she did not come back to life. A gentleman came soon after to confirm the death of Francesca, and she was to go identify the body. She was in shock. She still believed she was alive and in the hospital, but she was not. The death of her daughter was a new reality. I was amazed at the love, and smile on this woman's face when she spoke of her daughter. She seemed to be in acceptance of her death, however, there were pockets of suppressed emotions mixed together inside of her heart. There was also guilt that the father of their daughter dressed her with, which brought up more pain from that of their past relationship together. We addressed these feelings and also her challenges in driving near or past the beach where her daughter breathed her final breath these past years prior. She was somewhat haunted by the visual of the accident scene in her mind with the police scene and the yellow caution tape and imagining her daughter being thrown to her death. We then meditated together. My intent was to leave her with a tool that she could use to evolve herself spiritually and bring her peace. I offered her a way to meditate that could perhaps become her practice of 'no more struggle'. She seemed lifted as she participated willingly and with a heartwarming openness that I admired in her. I am grateful for the afternoon we shared together, and trust she is becoming a light for others.

After the Newness wore off

I had an amazing opportunity to interview a bright young woman who I will call Jane. At the approximate age of six, her mother fell in love with a man from another country which resulted in a separation and divorce between her parents. She recalled that suddenly she was in a hearing with all these people that her dad had rallied together to show and tell the judge why she should stay with the father in the United States. After a year or so of Jane traveling back and forth to see her mother, she started to feel her absence. "After the newness wore off, reality set in," she said. This resulted in her experiencing stomach issues, and what teachers in school called "her mysterious illness." Some years went by, and her mom planned to return home to the United States the winter that Jane turned twelve. "The day I told mom that dad got engaged, was the same day my mom said she was coming

home," Jane said. She went on to share how she remembered
her father was very strict about the custody arrangements for
her mother's return and recalls him saying, "You are not going to interrupt the nice thing we have going on here" to her
mom. Jane was upset. There were so many changes in her
life situations at that time. This parallels many children's stories, including that of my own child's. There are so many
changes that occur in their life circumstances that it creates a
lot of potential suffering for children. Jane went on to say, "I
felt guilty about my dad trying to make us into a family unit
with his new marriage. Which is what I wanted...but I had a
hard time balancing that with the desire to be with my mom."
I asked why she felt a family with siblings was important.
She replied, "I felt it was making up for what I didn't have. I
felt I deserved that life."

When Jane turned seventeen, she said she became
more rebellious and didn't care about anything. This tumbled
her into different life situations and choices she made
throughout the next years. She shared these experiences with
me. These experiences included more separation. The separation of a lover, and the death of her step-mom. She
experienced much loss and much sudden change. When she

began to speak of her current partner, her eyes smiled as she told me what she loved about him and her relationship with him. I asked her what she loved about herself. She replied, "I am trying to figure that out. That's a good question." I asked if she could separate herself from her roles like that of a mother, an expecting mother, a girlfriend, a daughter, a student...and put a space around it all, would she be able to find herself in that space? She said, "Yes. Once I create the space." She said that she will find that out when she gets her degree. "Oh? So who you are is another role?" I asked. She pondered this. We went on to discuss the 'you' beyond the 'you'. I wanted to introduce her to the 'I am' of who she truly is.

I began to discuss the concept of the inner child within her, and introduced her to the idea of being in spiritual matrimony with that inner child, and letting go of her past pain. She replied, "If I can let it go, maybe." I asked her to take the 'if' away. If is fear. Fear doesn't even exist. Only in the mind. I told her to begin with the awareness that she has the pain, that it is still there and it is okay. Then surrender to it. To surrender to it is to give it up. Give it up to the Universe. To God. To the nothingness of all things that are transient.

To all of these external transient situations. Does this mean harboring it a dock? No. Release it from the dock. Untie the boat and surrender it to the ocean. Surrender it and let it go. "I like that. It's a peaceful thought when you put it that way" she said. We went on in a deeper discussion and she concluded that she is no longer living in fear that something bad is going to happen.

I honor her enormously for this and know she is taking brave and enormous strides toward self-love. I trust that she understands now, the importance of self-love and how it affects her well-being in body, mind, and spirit. Although her story differs from yours and mine, it still shares the same essence of loss and separation. It still speaks of pain that derives from it all. The question is: Can you learn to navigate through your own life situations and not lose your truth, your 'self' in this world we call life?

You have just heard three different stories from three different people, and yet they all shared the same thing. Pain. Can you see how there is a connection between compassion and pain? This sense of mutuality in the experience of pain can be self-transforming. It is this shared humanity that brings an openness to our own pain that always asks, "Where can I grow from here?" The growth comes from how we learn to transmute this pain into peace. That is the end of suffering. When we can say yes to what is, we can come into peace.

"Is it possible for you to surrender it all?"
~Lily Sanders

CHAPTER 18

Saying Yes to What Is

SAYING YES TO WHAT IS, will put you in the present moment. Being in the present moment will keep you here, and not over there. This is the ultimate goal. The goal is to be here, which takes your mind off past occurrences and away from future fears that only exist in the mind. What is the commentary going on in your mind? Do you know? Are you even aware? Sometimes there is so much chatter going on that it becomes a background static that you grow accustomed to. Disengage with the mental dialogue, because it will never bring you peace. Rather be in acceptance of what is, at this very moment, and say yes to it. This will bring you into presence and end the suffering. Remember, the suffering is mental. You read of my experiences and that of others. You also have your own sad and woeful stories from your personal past experiences. Is it possible for you to surrender it all?

If I had not learned to love myself and understand the amazing power and loving life that the present moment offers, then I would have remained imprisoned in the emotional and mental warfare that was going on my head. The battle between me and the thoughts in my head was literally keeping me in the killing fields of life. Darting one mine, and getting blown up from the next. This is one way to live, but it is not *the* way to live. We are not here on a pointless journey to suffer. People often say, it never ends. I say, yes it does. But you need to make the choice to end it. And that choice begins with your choice for love.

At this point in the book, we know that we come to a state of calm when we are in acceptance of what is. We also know that we cannot change anything that has happened thirty years ago or even one minute ago. If this is so, then you may be wondering, if I cannot change what happened, how is that supposed to bring me peace? Peace comes from what you *can* change. So, what can you change? You can change the way you think about something that happened and not judge it. You can change the stronghold it has on you by letting it go. You can change your thoughts completely by setting your mind on the present moment. Surrender the wars of the mind that are robbing your peace. This is not a war worthy of your attention, or your heart. Place your attention on the light. When you raise the blinds, the light will come in.

When we experience loss, tragedy, or despair in our life, we typically store it in our mental warehouse. We keep the past experience alive, and continuously relate with it as we master warehouse management. We pull things from this aisle and stack things in the next. We keep the denser items at the bulk ends for quick and easy access, and to remind us that they are there. But these things we store in our mental warehouse are illusory and only exist in the mind. Remember, this is what keeps you in suffering mode. Isn't it about time that you accept what is, address all of your past pain, and release all thoughts and judgments of it in your mind, into the nothingness from which it came? Remember, to release a past experience means to let go of the commentary in your mind about it. Because this is the added story that brings you into suffering. When you can let go of the commentary in the mind, peace will shine through. This is the promise of presence. Release the suffering in your mind. Let go of the judgment and self-judgment, blame and self-blame, anger and rage, and all of the other useless things that your thoughts have been feeding you. None of this nourishes the soul, and all of it keeps you from peace. You are so deserving of having love and peace in your life. In my view, it is our birthright. Claim it. Take charge of life by giving up the battle between your thoughts and reality. Surrender to the battle of the mind and lay your beautiful head on the loving fields of peace.

Once you are in this space of peace, you can begin to sense a new energy that vibrates in and around you. Utilize that energy and vibration to serve your highest Self. When I speak of a higher Self, I speak of the intensity, greatness, and strength that you truly are in your connection with Oneness. Always remember that you are well-connected, most significant and eternally loved.

CHAPTER 19

The Crucifier

THE CRUCIFIER. EVERYONE HAS ONE. Perhaps this sounds crazy, but consider it for a moment. Is there one person in your past or current life experiences that seem to never let up on you? It is as if that person made an unconscious lifetime vow to bleed you out until the day one of you leaves this earth. You know this person. This is the unconscious human that shows up unannounced every time you let your spiritual guard down. No matter where you are, this person enters in like a thief in the night attempting to rob your joy every time you forget that you are a worthy, beautiful, loving, and conscious soul. This is your crucifier.

For some, their crucifier is someone none other than them self and may manifest as an addiction or a strong sense of emotional self-condemnation. As for me, I grew from my

crucifier. Who would have known that this person's unconscious actions were to bring me closer to my soul's journey?
All of it has given me an amazing spiritual outcome. Every
unconscious ball thrown my way have become learning
curves, and today, have grounded me at soul level. This was
a massive change from the ungrounded tortured soul I imagine he knew years ago. Because of this self-transformation, I
expect all of the unconscious actions, as hateful as they seem,
to be nothing less than Divine. Why? Because it has made
me an integrated expression of who I am. It seems that the
crucifier triggers us into releasing that which stops us from
living our truth. It allows us to be painfully honest with ourselves and how we feel about a situation. It also invites us to
do a self-inquiry. And in that self-inquiry, can you exercise
love and acceptance for all that is, and still rise above the
chaos of dark energy? Can you walk in the light and love
someone you completely disagree with? Of course, you can.

As for me, there is one thing I know. There is nothing
anyone's actions can do that will ever have power over me or
the joy in this moment. It can only illuminate me more. Dark
energy is powerless as it dwells in the shadows of the light. I
have woken up, as I listen to and heed to what innate tells me.

It always speaks when I am present. To me, being present is being tuned in. With this new fine tuning, I can create the experiences I want, with loving people surrounding me. If you can clearly see in your mind's eye your dreams, and vibrate with the frequency of having those dreams, you can attract everything you desire.

I discussed energy and vibration within the pages of this book a lot. Situations like dealing with someone who is constantly crucifying you are no different. Don't lower the standard of your energy. Instead, raise the bar. Heighten the vibration on earth by radiating your highest vibration out there, instructing the world in form to reflect it back to you. Allow the world to match your loving light energy to yours. Not the other way around. Reverse the flow of energy by letting your highest vibrational energy dominate all situations. Be soulful, and know your Oneness with Divinity so that you no longer match and mirror the collective unconsciousness. Adopt a soulful approach to all of your life situations. Remember, our soul is nourished by what it gives out. Not by what it receives. So go out there and be the expression of love and light that you were purposed to be, and use this light to help you navigate through every life situation. Never forget who you are. You *are*. And you are loved.

As for me, I triumphed. It has all been a win. None of what happened in the past matters. The only thing that matters is how I learned to navigate through life situations without sacrificing my truth. Who I am. I will no longer be the person that allows people to hurt me, and I will no longer hurt others. Instead, I allow unconscious actions to afford me the opportunity to love myself and my inner child even more. I remain present and tuned in. Imagine the peace and power in that? In my view, turning the other cheek takes on a whole new meaning when you have truly awakened. It doesn't mean you are giving up your power. It doesn't mean you are to be someone's doormat, either. It means quite the opposite. It means that you are taking your power back. Bless them and send them away from your front door. Their dark energy is no longer welcomed. But you do it with a soulful approach. Do it in love, not weakness. Don't misinterpret love for weakness. Love is never weak. I cannot express this enough. Love is the strongest energy of all existence. Nothing can destroy it. No energy is stronger than Love. This is your truth.

Practice breathing through the vibration of your highest self, and you will no longer be a victim of someone else's pain or your own for that matter. Past experiences do not define who you are. They never did. It was only your unconscious mind that convinced you of this. Now is the time to make the conscious shift. I encourage you to go deeper than your thinking mind and begin to feel and act out, at soul level. This shift is what I have discussed throughout this book. The shift from unconscious to conscious, from form into formless, from darkness into the light. This light is Love. Your truth. Your triumph. Welcome home. I love you.

Notes

Cinderella as told by Paul Tripp
RCA Camden (songs by Anne and Milton Delugg)

Scripture quotations marked (NIV) are taken from the Holy Bible, New International Version®, NIV®. Copyright © 1973, 1978, 1984, 2011 by Biblica, Inc.™ Used by permission of Zondervan. All rights reserved worldwide. www.zondervan.com The "NIV" and "New International Version" are trademarks registered in the United States Patent and Trademark Office by Biblica, Inc.™

Excerpt of Proceedings
Minutes of Stipulation and Order
Supreme Court of the State of New York
County of Suffolk

Case Study (US Experiment on Infants Withholding Affection)
tpauls.vxcommunity.com/Issue/Us-Experiment-On-Infants-Withholding-Affection/13213

HeartMath Institute (expanding heart connections)
Neurocardiology: Anatomical and Functional Principles
By J. Andrew Armour, M.D., Ph.D.

Disclaimer

This book is designed to provide inspiration, insight, perspective, and potential guidance to those readers who have an interest in spiritual growth. This text should only be used as a general guide and not as the ultimate source for spiritual growth and self-help. The author and ABL Publishing shall have neither liability nor responsibility to any person or entity with respect to any loss or damage caused, directly or indirectly, by the information contained in this book.

ABL Publishing
71 Broadway
New York, N.Y.10006

Our publishing mission is to spread love and raise the vibration of collective consciousness around the globe.

If you have interest in seeing more of our products and ordering additional copies of this publication please e-mail at ABLpublishing@outlook.com

To subscribe to Lily Sanders' newsletters, stay informed of speaking events, and for booking engagements please e-mail at   Lily@ueslifecoach.com

We are blessed to stay connected with you!

"Love is the essence of all consciousness. Love is the stimulus for everything in life. It is the yeast that develops and gives rise to our daily bread."

~Lily Sanders